Traeger

THE PEDAL RADIO MAN

He Gave A Voice To The Bush
And To Flying Doctors

FRED McKAY

Cover Picture: Alfred Traeger and original pedal wireless. (See Chapter 6.)
Cover Illustration: Bush scene of the Flying Doctor. Dr Russell-Weisz (Broken Hill) discusses the immunisation plans with Fred McKay for a group of children who have gathered from their homes.

First published in 1995 by Boolarong Press

National Library of Australia
Cataloguing-in-Publication data

McKay, James Frederick, 1907- .
Traeger, the pedal radio man: he gave a voice to the bush and to flying doctors.

Bibliography.
ISBN 0 86439 192 7.

1. Traeger, Alfred Hermann, 1895-1980. 2. Royal Flying Doctor Service of Australia. 3. Radio engineers – Australia – Biography. 4. Radio – Australia – History. I. Title.

621.384092

BOOLARONG PRESS
1/655 Toohey Road, Salisbury, Qld 4107 Australia.
www.boolarongpress.com.au
Design and phototypesetting by
Ocean Graphics Pty Ltd, Gold Coast, Qld.
Printed and bound by Watson Ferguson & Company, Brisbane.

Contents

Appreciation

Storry Walton, the Public Affairs Manager of the Australian Council of the Royal Flying Doctor Service, has been the motivating influence and the practical encourager behind the total plan to tell the story of Alfred Traeger.

Technical information has come from the radio researcher and friend Mervyn Eunson of Brisbane, who has taken professional delight in destroying certain myths that have gathered around the early history of Traeger and his ingenious work.

Joyce Traeger Blaess of Adelaide, highly respected widow of Alfred Traeger, has shown special grace in giving access to personal family letters and photographs.

Valued contributions have been made by George Wilson (Flying Doctor Author), Graham Schultz (Glenlee family), Richard Woldendorp (Photographer), Allan Aldridge (Photographer), Tom Moore (Artist), Bill Batten (Mapping), Lester Padman and Russell Keirnan (Boolarong Press) and Maisie McKenzie (Consulting Author).

Margaret McKay has gladly given patient hours at an old-fashioned typewriter.

An intriguing input has come from 87 people in various parts of Australia who, in response to the A.B.C. programmes 'Australia All Over (Ian McNamara) and 'Summer All Over (Colin Munro), have sent messages by telephone and letters with important information about Traeger and with a whole range of suggested titles for his story. This was a source of unexpected and warm-hearted helpfulness.

Preface

Alfred Hermann Traeger was the kind of person whose life story is best told as a fireside yarn.

Therefore no attempt is made to write a definitive biography or even a structured history.

Traeger discovered the meaning of his life when travelling along lonely outback tracks. He loved the smell of gum trees on the banks of meandering bush creeks. He found a strange happiness in giving what he called 'a big surprise' to isolated families in the Never Never who were completely cut off from the rest of the world. He gave them the miracle pedal radio so that they could call the Flying Doctor. And he kept on bringing the benefits of wireless to people of the bush all his life.

His workshop was no palace. He didn't require a palace. All he needed was a decent workbench on which to fashion his ingenious machines. Then he went outback again in the loaded Dodge Buckboard.

He was driven by a deep inner compelling spirit. He had a great practical vision. It was the same kind of goal that drove his boss, Flynn of the Inland, into action.

The story of this book is therefore unadorned and simple.

Traeger was a revolutionary. And he didn't know it.

Introduction

It happened on the dry tree-lined banks of the Cloncurry River in North Western Queensland. I had pulled up in my truck to unroll my swag and boil the billy. It was the 10th February 1937.

I hastened to rig up my new mobile pedal wireless set. It had arrived from Adelaide the day before in an oblong pine box at the Cloncurry Railway Station. I unwound the aerial and threw it over a high branch of the nearby gum and tied the counterpoise to a shovel fixed in the ground about 15 metres away. I was nervous as I sat on my tucker box with my feet on the twin pedals of the generator.

As I pedalled I grasped the microphone and called up the mother station of the Flying Doctor Service. "VJI, VJI," I repeated. "This is 8YS Portable calling . . . Can you hear me? Over."

Everyone in the Outback knew Maurie Anderson's voice. He was the head wireless man at the Flying Doctor Radio Base. He spoke in a drawling, friendly voice. On this occasion, however, he spluttered with excitement. "VJI replying," he almost shouted. "Fred, you've made it! Your signal is loud and clear. Congratulations." I wanted to talk on, but Maurie Anderson had a bundle of other urgent traffic to handle. I knew also that I had to get used to saving precious time on the Flying Doctor Network.

I muttered something to myself. "This is a blinking miracle," I quietly added. A solitary kookaburra laughed from somewhere down the creek.

The story I am attempting to tell is about the radio amateur Alfred Traeger whose ingenuity made this whole thing possible. He gave a voice to the silent bush, and in practical terms saved the Reverend John Flynn from failure in his dreams about flying doctors.

At this point I have to stop and make a youthful confession. The very first official radio message I sent next morning was to a trainee nurse at the General Hospital in Brisbane – over 700 kilometres away. Everybody in the bush heard my telegram because in pedal radio country there were no secrets.

My mates on a cattle station halfway up Cape York Peninsula never allowed me to forget the fun they got out of listening to that first special communication I sent into the open skies. No wonder. My pedal wireless radiogram arrived in Brisbane with this romantic message: "The longest and most loving kiss you have ever received is sent by pedal radio from a creek bank near Cloncurry."

Margaret Robertson was the girl I had left behind when I set out from Brisbane a year before, and whom I had farewelled at the back gate of the Brisbane General Hospital, not to see her again for at least two years or more.

"It happened on the dry tree-lined banks of the Cloncurry River . . . . the very first official radio message I sent was to a trainee nurse at the General Hospital in Brisbane – 700 kilometres away."

This vibrant young brunette was to share my swag as my wife when her nursing training was completed. She was to travel the back blocks with me in a one-tonne truck. On the roadside she was to become a skilled operator of the portable pedal radió. And on a never-to-be-forgotten, disastrous breakdown accident on a forlorn track near the top corner of the Simpson Desert she was to weep tears of joy when, after three days, our pedal wireless SOS call brought a life-saving rescuing party.

The plain fact is that I of all people have a personal right to thank God for the man who invented and constructed my mobile pedal radio.

Therefore the story I tell of this quietly spoken, and utterly shy, young man is no fairy tale. Alfred Traeger is part of the social history of Outback Australia, and thousands of people owe him a debt immeasurable.

FRED McKAY
Hawkesbury Village
Richmond NSW

Dedication

Dedicated to the memory of Maurie Anderson and Vernon Kerr, the radio operators at the pioneer aerial medical base in Cloncurry who taught me the technical mysteries of Traeger's pedal wireless, and also in tribute to their successors in the various radio bases of the Royal Flying Doctor Service throughout Australia who have been the vital life-saving communicators behind the scene.

Maurice Bernard Anderson 1908-60

The wizard radio 'ham' Maurie Anderson, Traeger's pioneering colleague, was chief operator of the original Flying Doctor base in Cloncurry for nine years. He also opened the Alice Springs base in 1939, and served with Distinction as a Radio Officer in the North Australian Observations Unit during World War II. He died of a severe tropical illness contracted on active service.

– CHAPTER ONE –

A Farmer's Son With New Ideas

His trousers were held up with a pair of striped braces. He stood, a spare physical frame, 170 centimetres in height. Open shirt. Tousled black hair. A slightly tanned face with clear brown eyes. A quiet friendly voice.

From boyhood he looked what he really was – the son of an everyday farmer. However, at six years of age, he began to show a dislike of milking yards and chicken pens. His parents were puzzled. From the beginning, the family livelihood had been on the land. This youngster had a strange new bent.

At 12 years of age he astonished the local farmers by building a telephone line from the family dwelling to the implement shed 50 metres away. With inventive imagination he made the magnet for the improvised telephone unit out of the prongs of a hay pitchfork, and he collected tobacco tin lids to fabricate the necessary diaphragms for the peculiar device, while he broke up charcoal from the kitchen stove to provide the carbon granules for the awkward-looking microphone. Everyone laughed. But the amazing contraption did work in a fashion!

His father, increasingly aware of the boy's unusual talents, enrolled him at 16 in the four-year course in Mechanical and Electrical Engineering at the Adelaide School of Mines and Industry.

During his 20th year, in mid-term while he was completing his Diploma Certificate, he was madly reading about fellow German Heinrich Hertz and the great Marconi and their stunning experiments with electromagnetic waves. For his practical examination, however, he was allotted the task of making a small high-tension generator. Electric gadgets became his hobby. His kitbag began to bulge with coils of copper wire, carbon brushes, magnets and armature loops.

The Traeger Family (Circa 1908)
From Left: Hedwig Louise, Johann Hermann (Father), Johann Gustav, Alfred Hermann, Pauline Louise (Mother), Matilda Louise.

Interestingly enough, during the last six months of his course at the Adelaide School of Mines he and some of his young friends also got mixed up with the extraordinary happenings that were taking place among the radio amateurs ('hams') who were starting to send Morse-coded shortwave messages to other 'hams' all over Australia. He too put together a radio transmitter of his own, and three months before completing the Electrical Engineering Diploma Course he was sending Morse code at 20 words a minute and hoping to work toward his Amateur Radio Licence.

His first full-time job was in the Adelaide Tramways Workshop. Then he had a stint in the General Post Office as a mechanic and telegraphist.

When he turned 27 he daringly set up his own small electrical business, firstly in a room at the back of the family home where he lived with his parents, who had come from the farm at Balaclava to the Adelaide suburb of Kensington Gardens.

Hannan Brothers, the well-known firm who ran the popular garage and service station in Wakefield Street, Adelaide, offered him the job of electrical mechanic in their main workshop. Winding and servicing generators for cars and trucks at Hannan Brothers Garage – between times getting a lot of fun in developing his special hobby as a radio 'ham' – and going to the local Lutheran Church with his parents, his two sisters and brother Jack on Sundays – this was his life.

At 30, in Hannan's workshop he still looked like a working hand from a wheat farm – unconcerned about social life, content with his daily work, unpretentious, of very shy disposition, and virtually unknown.

His name was Alfred Hermann Traeger. A farmer's son with new ideas.

CHAPTER TWO

A Bush Parson With New Ideas

This man had the appearance of a city gentleman in his dark suit and waistcoat. It was the way he had been brought up, the son of a professional teacher in the Victorian Education Department. When he became a Minister in the Presbyterian Church he went to the faraway backblocks of inland Australia. He was a practical man with a restless, sensitive spirit.

As he travelled the distant Never Never tracks he sensed a deep feeling of distress as he came face to face with the frightening hardships that were an inescapable part of the day-to-day lives of these people. He wrote articles about the 'Dread of Isolation' – the loneliness, the insecurity, no next-door neighbours, no community life. There were scattered graves of young stockmen who should not have died, and of mothers and their babies. These were the grim facts of life as he found them in the Australian bush.

It was surprising that the son of a reserved schoolmaster should be the one to dream about new and outlandish schemes to help these faraway people. He started to talk about a fresh approach to Christian ministry in the inland by patrolling padres who would build no churches but mooch up and down every outback track on their camels or horses, sharing the everyday battles of lonely people. He next confounded his colleagues by enlisting teams of women to go to this rough untamed land, young well-trained nurses, to set up bush hospitals in out-of-the-way places.

"He went to the faraway places of inland Australia".

His haunting dream, however, went much further. He had 'a fire in his belly' about the creation of a scheme of flying doctors to bring medical security to the entire Australian frontier country.

But the agonising gap in this man's visionary hopes was the tragic absence of any known method by which the people in distant and scattered parts of Australia could even talk with one another, let alone call up a Sky Doctor when the need arose.

A very close and understanding friend, David Wyles, who was a senior staff member of Philips Lamps Coy Ltd in Sydney, hinted to this bush parson that it may be worthwhile doing some research in the field of radio.

The bush parson was no dullard. He knew too truly that to build telephone lines to cover the tremendous and treeless distances in the bush was in practical terms totally out of the question, so he set his mind immediately on discovering what every wireless manual could teach him.

And he became as skilled in this field as any general amateur, finally being welcomed into the select fraternity of the Wireless Institute of Australia. Here he had contact with retired Army Officer George Towns, a radio enthusiast who in the beginning felt that the dreams of this visionary clergyman were impossible but finally ended up by helping him to fulfill them!

The outback adventures of George Towns came when he offered to go with this bush parson on a shared road trip to experiment with selected radio equipment under real inland conditions. Towns gave expert assistance in Sydney in assembling the necessary radio gear and in purchasing two commercially built generators to provide the electric power for transmitting. The total equipment was boxed and despatched by rail to Adelaide, where a new Dodge Buckboard (a well-type utility truck) was on order at Weymouth Motors.

Before departing on the venturing trip to the isolated country around Innamincka and Birdsville in the laden Dodge Buckboard, the fateful discovery was made that the two generators from Sydney were totally unsatisfactory. This meant that there was no source of electrical power for the radio transmitter and that therefore the whole venture for the time being had to be cancelled.

The bush parson with the new ideas was the unpredictable John Flynn of the Australian Inland Mission. He lit his pipe and pondered, "Where in Australia can I find the necessary high-voltage generator that I just have to have?".

CHAPTER THREE

They Met In A Garage Workshop

Alfred Traeger got the surprise of his life. The Reverend John Flynn in his black suit rushed into the Mechanical Workshop at Hannan Brothers in Wakefield Street at 10 o'clock on the morning of 14th June 1925. Neither of them had ever seen or heard of the other. Traeger was flabbergasted.

Flynn stood at the bench where Traeger was working, and looking at him with a kind of desperation in his voice, asked bluntly, "Have you still got that generator?" "What generator?" Traeger asked in utter surprise. "The 600-volt one you had tested at the 5CL workshop a couple of months ago." "Yes, why?" Traeger answered with increasing astonishment. "How much do you want for it?" Flynn queried with a new sense of urgency in his voice.

Traeger was almost dumb. Scratching his head he slowly replied, "Oh – about £29/10/-." Flynn paid him in cash, and after staying for 15 minutes to explain what it was all about, carried the precious generator out to the car where George Towns was waiting. Neither Traeger nor Flynn imagined that they would ever meet again.

It was a curious meeting of these two very different people. George Towns had talked with Harry Kauper, the technical manager of radio station 5CL, about Flynn's proposed trip. When the problem about the urgently needed generator was discussed, Kauper explained that a young fellow named Traeger who worked at Hannan Brothers Garage had tested a 600-volt generator at the 5CL workshop

"Yes, I remember! I met him in a garage workshop!" – *Alfred Traeger speaking to the South Australian Governor on the day he received the O.B.E. decoration.*

a few months earlier. Kauper knew that this generator would exactly suit John Flynn's requirements for his bush experiments.

The loaded Dodge Buckboard car was an extraordinary sight as Flynn and Towns set out on their daring journey on the third week of June 1925.

Traeger's generator was fixed to the splashboard on the passenger side of the vehicle and a special pulley was mounted on the rear wheel which, when jacked up, could drive the generator by means of an attached belt. Flynn purchased long rolls of coir matting to get over the sandhills. The radio equipment included a 100-watt transmitter, using the 80-metre wavelength, extra accumulators, a supply of dry batteries, two shortwave receivers and a broadcast receiver. For the required aerial mast, four three-metre sections of light steel tube were strapped to the side of the truck with a timber jib and block and tackle to erect it.

The route was a 2,400-kilometre trek from Adelaide to Beltana, Innamincka, Birdsville, back to Marree, and ending up in Alice Springs. It proved an arduous, gruelling journey with chilling winter nights. Some of their transmission experiments had a degree of success even though it was impossible to procure a steady signal with the generator belt being driven from the jacked-up rear wheel of the Dodge Buckboard. But many lessons were learned. Flynn humorously talked about 'successful failures', and at least Morse code was proved to be the only option for reliable communication in the bush areas for the time being.

At Alice Springs, George Towns was compelled to return to Sydney owing to indifferent health, and Flynn was also forced to abandon his radio exploits until the next year, because the building, opening and staffing of the hospital in Alice Springs were tasks that demanded exhausting and full-time energies. Furthermore, there were critical meetings of his Australian Inland Mission in Melbourne in September 1926, and it wasn't until these administrative jobs were completed that he would at last be able to return to his

"Yes, I remember! He was one of my greatest discoveries!" – *Rev. John Flynn speaking to a reporter on his 70th birthday.*

"The loaded Dodge Buckboard was an extraordinary sight as George Towns and John Flynn set out on their daring journey."

wireless ventures, and to pick up the Dodge Buckboard, which he had left at Oodnadatta.

It was late September 1926 therefore before he caught the train from Melbourne to Adelaide. He made contact again with his friend Harry Kauper, who offered him the use of the 5CL workshop and so became the 'laboratory godfather' throughout the whole series of the radio experiments.

It was Kauper who suggested that Flynn needed a helper. "What about asking Alfred Traeger, the radio amateur who made the 600-volt generator?" And so the providential happening took place when Flynn turned up again at Hannan's Garage and offered Traeger the job at £6 (about $12) a week! Traeger said he would have come for half that pay! He had never dreamt of any proposal just like this one.

From that moment Flynn, Kauper and Traeger working together in the 5CL workshop became a dedicated trio, assembling two outpost sets and testing Edison copper oxide batteries for the provision of transmitting power. Ernest Fisk of A.W.A. in Sydney had advised the Australian Inland Mission Board in August 1926 that he was prepared to make a special gift of the experimental base station in Alice Springs. This was the outcome of Flynn's friendly strategy behind the scenes. In early September that year Fisk despatched to Adelaide the complete radio equipment for the Alice Springs base unit, and all that needed to be done was the installation of the power unit and aerial system.

Alfred Traeger seemed to be born for this hour. There was an inner sense of adventure in his bloodstream. He inherited the pioneering tradition of a well-known migrant German family in South Australia. They had selected and developed farming areas in the virgin country approximately 100 kilometres north of Adelaide. This original Schultz family (Alf's great-grandparents) had come by sailing ship from Hamburg with a group of fervent Evangelical Lutherans who were determined to start life anew in a country where they would have complete freedom to follow their religious beliefs without interference by any State authorities.

A daughter of the Schultz family married a young man from the next door farm called Gottlieb Traeger. Their son, Hermann Traeger, in turn married 21-year-old Louise Zerna from another nearby farm. This couple with German adventure in their blood decided to start their married life in a totally new area. They packed their goods in a four-wheel German wagon drawn by bullocks and set out on their long, slow, honeymoon trek to the Wimmera district in Victoria some 410 kilometres away. They finally took up a small farm at Glenlee in the Dimboola Shire. In their modest but comfortable home with one warming chimney, our Alfred Hermann Traeger was born on Saturday 2nd August 1895, and Aunt Bertha Cramer came by buggy from Ni Ni Well to act as midwife. Alf spent his boyhood up to the age of twelve on the Glenlee farm and went to the local school with his two older sisters and his younger brother. Life was simple, unworldly, but never dull.

Alf's mother was a typical, hard-working perfectionist whose discipline of the children, especially the boys, was what Alf later claimed to be 'strict and true'. Workdays on the farm and Sunday at church was the unbroken family ritual.

At the end of 16 years at Glenlee the family moved back to South Australia and settled on a section of the old Traeger farm at Balaclava for the next 10 years. Alf's father quickly realised that Alf had practically no interest in farming but was exhibiting his unusual bent for mechanics. The wise encouragement of both his father and mother made it possible for Alf to do the things he wanted to do at High School and the Adelaide School of Mines and when he reached 21 his father decided to find general employment for himself in the city and purchased a home in the Adelaide suburb of Kensington Gardens so that the career opportunities of

Memorial at Traeger's birthplace – Glenlee, Victoria.

the 'children' could be extended. So it happened that Alfred Hermann Traeger became a well-furnished electrical engineer winding generators in Hannan's Garage. The unexpected adventure of going to Alice Springs with Rev. John Flynn was exciting.

There was also a degree of quiet religious zeal behind Traeger's enthusiasm. At Sunday School he had heard stories of the Lutheran missionaries at Hermannsburg Aboriginal Mission, and he was aware from his discussions with John Flynn that one of the experimental baby wireless sets was to be installed there. Another bonus – he would be able to help the work of his own Church!

In October 1926 Alf joined Flynn on the train to Oodnadatta. The two wooden cases continuing the wireless gear were in the guard's van with the 18 glass Edison batteries. John Flynn was tired and slept most of the journey, while Traeger's eager eyes scanned the changing sights of the passing countryside. He saw Afghans on loaded camels at Marree for the first time, kangaroos hopping out of the awful dust storm near Beltana, and bushmen with wide hats around the popular pub at William Creek.

At Oodnadatta A.I.M. Nursing Home, the nursing sisters filled their tucker-box with beef and homemade bread. The trip to Alice Springs in the Dodge Buckboard was a bit baffling for the new traveller as they battled with sand crossings, sweltering heat and hordes of persistent flies!

By 20th October 1926 Traeger had a comfortable bed on the verandah of the new A.I.M. Nursing Home in Alice Springs, the guest of the two caring nursing sisters, Nell Small and Ina Pope.

Alice Springs was at the end of the Centralian road – a small but sturdy trading village of about 100 people served mostly by camel teams. Traeger wandered up the lonely main street. He talked to Bill Littlejohn the policeman. There was a feeling of excitement in the air. He was in the very heart of the Continent. And for him a completely unknown journey ahead.

CHAPTER FOUR

"The Light On The Hill"

It was the 11th November 1926. Flynn and Traeger were up early to travel in the cool of the morning. The Dodge Buckboard had again been laden with wireless gear and aerial poles, but this time there were also nine heavy-duty glass Edison copper oxide batteries strapped together behind the cabin. Hermannsburg, about 130 kilometres west of Alice Springs, was their destination.

Traeger put up the first outback aerial mast at the rear of the A.I.M. Nursing Home in Alice Springs and in the engine room assembled the experimental mother station.

As the truck jolted on the rough track past Simpsons Gap and Standley Chasm, Traeger kept a careful eye on the radio equipment, which comprised a complete receiving and transmitting baby set that had been put together by Kauper in Adelaide, with Flynn at his side, and upon which the first critical experiment at Hermannsburg now depended. Traeger had already installed the 32-volt electric lighting plant in the engine room at the rear of the nursing home, driven by a five-horsepower Lister engine. This provided the power to operate the 50-watt mother station, firstly to carry out the telephony experiments on 88 metres with the baby sets, and secondly to operate an auxiliary Morse code unit to contact Kauper in Adelaide.

Traeger couldn't hide his glee when Kauper gave his glowing report on the reception in Adelaide. 8AB, the Alice Springs mother station, was now successfully on the air, and Traeger couldn't stop Flynn talking about the next part of the experiment and the fun they were going to have in teaching the Hermannsburg people to learn Morse code in operating their baby set.

As they drove through the entry gate at Hermannsburg, Pastor Frederick Wilhelm Albrecht, the Missioner, came to meet them. With him were two wide-eyed black men who were thoroughly mystified by the strangely loaded vehicle. A noisy group of Aboriginal children gathered round as Mr. Albert Heinrich, the Mission school teacher, rang the bell for the midday break. Traeger was enjoying every moment of this new experience, and an Aboriginal youngster about nine years of age started to follow him around wherever he went. This lad, Edwin Pareroultja, in later life became one of the Albert Namatjira school of painters capturing in water-colour the wonderful landscape pictures of the McDonnell Ranges. As a shirtless boy in khaki pants he developed a kind of soul mateship with the 'radio man', and eventually continued this bond of friendship all his life, because Traeger was to make radio visits to Hermannsburg again and again in the years ahead.

The Alice Springs mother station 8AB. The total radio equipment for this experimental base station was donated by Ernest Fisk of Australian Amalgamated Wireless.

Traeger himself later admitted that his radio work at Hermannsburg brought a new dimension into the meaning of his career, and that Flynn's wireless dream had completely captured him, especially when he witnessed the joy and gratitude of the Aboriginal people, and even of the nine-year-old boy Edwin Pareroultja, who wanted to sleep beside him at night!

By the end of the first day at Hermannsburg the radio mast had been erected, and Flynn, with the mission carpenter, had fossicked around to find old pine boxes to make a table for the baby set. When night came Flynn talked for long hours with Pastor Albrecht while Traeger kept on tinkering by lamplight with the aerials and connections to the bank of Edison batteries.

On the early morning of 13th November Traeger without ceremony took his seat at the wireless table in the office of the mission store. All was ready for a scheduled call to Alice Springs where Maurie Fuss, a young operator from the telegraph station, had volunteered to man the mother base in the engine room of the nursing home. According to Flynn's well-laid plans, official approval had been given by Mr. James Malone, Manager of the Radio Branch of the Post Master General's Department, for radio transmission experiments to be carried out in the Alice Springs area with agreed call signs. The mother set in Alice Springs was powered to send its messages by voice, while the outstation sets had the capacity to transmit only in Morse code.

The time came for Traeger to make the scheduled call. He switched on the transmitter and with his right hand started to send 'dits' and 'dahs' on the Morse key. Then he stopped and turned on the receiver to listen for a reply from the

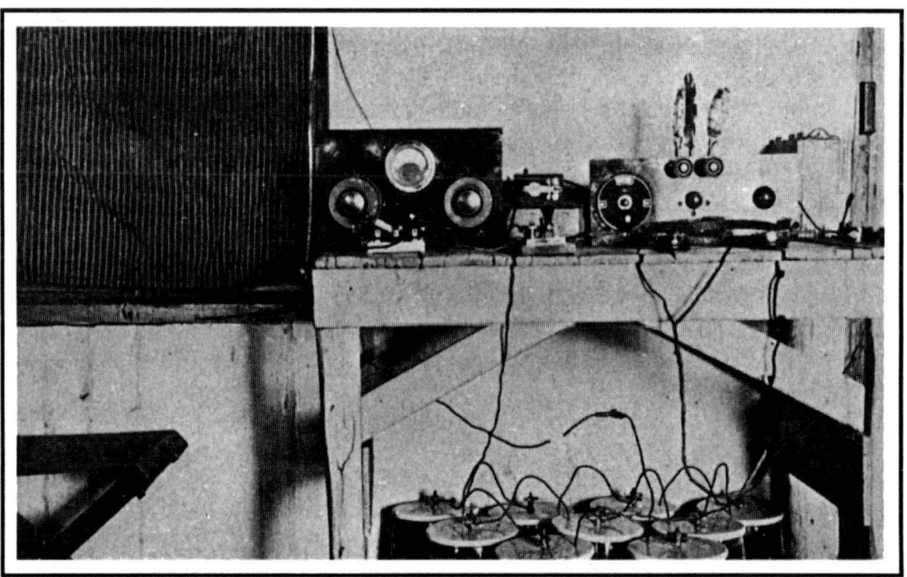

The first experimental baby set as installed at Hermannsburg (8AC). A similar set was installed at Arltunga (8AD). These sets were assembled by Traeger, Flynn and Kauper in the 5CL workshop in Adelaide.

mother station. Traeger was bewildered. There was no reply. He called again on the Morse key. Nothing.

In later years Alf Traeger spoke of the baffling disappointment of that moment because Pastor Albrecht and John Flynn were standing at his side, while Mr. Heinrich and the schoolchildren were pushing in at the door. Traeger was puzzled, but he was certain in his own mind that some problem had arisen at the Alice Springs end.

Flynn and Traeger stayed an additional five days with their new found and welcoming friends at Hermannsburg. Pastor Albrecht practised sending Morse code each day under Traeger's patient tuition and the final touches were made to the radio installation and the aerials. This also gave the opportunity for Alf to learn some Aranda words from his young friend Edwin and to sit beside him at the daily morning devotions that were held in the little Mission church.

The Dodge Buckboard got on the road again after the week's stay at Hermannsburg. Traeger arranged that he would give a radio call to Pastor Albrecht at five o'clock that day after their arrival back in Alice Springs.

That was another traumatic moment. Traeger quickly discovered that Maurie Fuss had inserted the wrong coil in the receiver of the Alice Springs set. Alf quickly made the change. John Flynn sat on a box in the engine room. His face gleamed with his typical grin as he listened to Pastor Albrecht sending his erratic Morse code in reply to Traeger's call. Although the experimental equipment was understandably unrefined and unwieldy and the Edison batteries were cumbersome and costly, the fact remained that a triumph in bush communication by radio had been achieved.

After the other baby set was successfully installed at Arltunga Police Station, about 150 kilometres east of Alice Springs, the twin outposts 8AC and 8AD began a daily schedule with the mother station 8AB.

A simple experimental scheme of radio contact between a mother station and two baby outposts in the bush was a reality.

An unofficial telegram was actually sent by Pastor Albrecht to his wife with her new baby in Tanunda near Adelaide, the message being sent in Morse code from Hermannsburg to the engine room behind the Alice Springs Nursing Home, and then transmitted to Tanunda as a regular telegram from the Post Office. That happened on 25th November 1926, John Flynn's 46th birthday.

The whole Alice Springs experiment was to Alfred Traeger a kind of 'light on the hill' – a sure glimmer of things to come once he got back to his workshop for further hard work.

CHAPTER FIVE

"Take Me To Cloncurry"

By the first week of December 1926, following the hopeful experiments at Alice Springs, Traeger had loaded the Dodge Buckboard again as he and John Flynn headed for the road back to Oodnadatta and Adelaide.

After his return to Sydney Flynn wrote two official reports describing the discovery that had been made in successful radio communication between the two distant outposts and the mother station. In spite of the technical importance of these reports, however, Flynn admitted that the greatest happening on the Alice Springs trip was his 'discovery' of Alfred Traeger, who had all the promise of being the kind of 'wireless wizard' who could carry forward with the urgent and innovative work still to be faced. Traeger himself realised that the Alice Springs experiment had opened up the way for continuous wave transmission in the bush, but he was also unmistakably aware that the banks of wet batteries and the cumbersome equipment used at Hermannsburg and Arltunga were quite out of the question for practical use in the scattered station homesteads.

The Australian Inland Mission Board agreed to Flynn's urgent recommendation that Traeger, the man who looked like a farming lad, be appointed as the Radio Engineer of the organisation. The far-seeing Flynn specified that Traeger be paid the same salary as he himself was receiving.

Following the hot and strenuous weeks in Alice Springs Alf was relieved to get out of working clothes and put on his Sunday suit for the church service on Christmas Day with his parents, two sisters and brother Jack. Family and Church loyalties in accordance with the strong Lutheran practice of the time were part of Alfred Traeger's life for the whole of his 85 years.

It became evident that as Alf set out to work day and night in his home workshop he had caught the urgency of the challenge of Flynn's dream. And now that he was compelled to wear brown-rimmed spectacles he joked about his likeness to Marconi!

On New Year's Day 1927 Traeger had purchased his first fountain pen. Letter writing up to this time had never been an exciting exercise for him, but in the period February-August of that year he developed the habit of putting on paper the things he was doing in his workshop. He wrote letter upon letter to Flynn explaining how he had tested an alternator from an old telephone and then had produced a contraption from an emery grinder with a specially wound mini-generator in place of the emery wheel. He described the endless hours he was spending in making completely new and smaller receiving and transmitting sets, and about Harry Kauper of 5CL helping him to incorporate 'crystal control' in the transmitter in order to maintain the wave-length at a fixed level even when the generator was driven at an uneven pace. Another improvement that Traeger outlined to Flynn was his new design of the aerial masts with tapering interlocking sections of piping used for bicycle frames. These 'reeds', as Flynn called them in his reply, would be lighter and more easily assembled for quick erection.

Meantime in Sydney Flynn was also keeping in regular touch with Ernest Fisk, the big man of A.W.A., who not only offered free technical advice but also provided radio parts at cost price. In addition, Mr. James Malone of the P.M.G. Radio Department showed encouraging practical interest in what Flynn was doing and responded to his overtures by granting official approval to carry out continuing experiments.

By the end of September 1927 Traeger had completed putting together what he believed would be a suitable transmitter-receiver baby set. It was ready for testing with a midget hand-driven generator. He literally pleaded with Flynn about the possibility of taking a road trip to Cloncurry to carry out urgently necessary trial runs. Dr. George Simpson and Rev. Andrew Barber had completed their survey of possible outback sites for the establishment of the pioneer Flying Doctor base, and Cloncurry in North West Queensland had been the unanimously selected township where Flynn's pioneering scheme would be tried out. Simpson and Barber, their task finished, had left Flynn's Dodge Buckboard in Rev. James Blake's care at the Presbyterian manse at Longreach. Early in October 1927 Traeger set off for Longreach by train with their radio equipment packed in two specially constructed cases. From the railhead he and Flynn in their beloved Dodge Buckboard were at last on their way to Cloncurry.

During the next two months Flynn and Traeger were together by themselves on the road. The track northward, right to Burketown, became their 'bush laboratory'. They brewed black tea in a billy can in lonely places, and on the grassy plains and in rocky gullies they stopped at selected spots to carry out radio experiments.

During the July-August period in Adelaide, Traeger had also written about his special device that embodied a hand-driven generator. He had talked with the manager of the Adelaide Foundry about the possibility of casting an outside structure for this new unit so that the winding operation by hand could be firm and steady for wireless transmission on the road.

This special piece of equipment became their 'secret weapon' on the journey from Longreach to Cloncurry. Flynn used to do the handwinding while Alf worked the Morse key. The operation was so successful that at Winton they booked in at the North Gregory Hotel and Flynn and Traeger got in a corner and discussed the possibility of making the hand-winding generator the standard method for supplying transmission power for the small outback sets. Alf was determined, however, to carry out experiments further north.

At Cloncurry there was no minister in the manse, but Traeger had his first opportunity of studying the available space in the church vestry and the general surroundings where the mother station and aerials would later be situated.

Traeger had an opportunity of studying the site where he would set up the first mother station. St. Cuthbert's Presbyterian Church, Cloncurry (rear view), with adjoining engine room for electric light plant.

Flynn had a further unannounced plan in his mind. He had written to Rev. R.H. Wilson, the Superintendent of Mornington Island Mission, and confirmed an arrangement for the Mission boat the *Morning Star* to be in Burketown on a certain date to enable him and Traeger to visit the Mornington Island community. They spent their first night in Cloncurry at the Post Office Hotel and next morning set off on their 'secret mission' northward. They had no intention of exhibiting the radio transmitter and equipment or carrying out any experiments on this journey, mainly because they felt that prospective lady operators at the station homesteads would be inclined to take fright when they saw that the Morse key was the only way to send messages!

"They made their first call at Augustus Downs." Mrs. Gertrude Rothery and children in front of the station homestead.

On the slow road they made their first call at Augustus Downs, about 300 kilometres from Cloncurry. Traeger knew that Flynn had planned, through Mr. Fred Brodie at Cloncurry, that this property would have the first outpost wireless when the scheme was set up. After dinner Mr. George Rothery, the manager, and his wife Gertrude were eagerly anxious to hear about the secret planning that was going on!

Before getting on the road next morning Flynn had the good fortune to meet Mr. Egerton Burnett from the next-door station Lorraine, who had driven his new Dodge car to Augustus Downs with the weekly mailbag. Traeger explained to Rothery and Burnett the wireless experiment that he and Flynn were developing to help people call up the Flying Doctor, and both men laughingly claimed "they had no time to learn blinkin' Morse code but their womenfolk would probably be game enough to give it a go!".

They moved on to Burketown, the small coastal village where the Leichhardt River runs into the waters of the Gulf of Carpentaria. Flynn drove straight to the police station where a special friend, Sergeant Jim Hosier, had already arranged to house the Dodge Buckboard while Flynn and Traeger boarded the waiting Mission boat, the *Morning Star*. The 130-kilometre journey to Mornington Island by Mission lugger gave Flynn the opportunity, between his attempts to sleep, to explain why he had selected Mornington Island as one of the first places for a Traeger Radio Set.

Mornington Island Mission had been established by the Presbyterian Church as a special endeavour to help the development of the well-known Lardil coastal group of Aboriginal people. In 1917 tragedy had come with the murder of the head Missionary, Rev. Richard Hall. The assistant Missionary was also critically injured. The wives of these two men with four children had been barricaded in their home for 10 days until the Mission launch came back from Burketown. It has been completely impossible throughout the whole tragic happening to make contact with the outside world. Flynn knew the details of this story and was a friend of Rev. R.H. Wilson, who had come from Kunmunya in Western Australia to rescue the situation. It was now Flynn's hope to give some practical help to his old friend in this isolated community.

Traeger was mesmerised by the whole scene, which was so different from the Aboriginal settlement at Hermannsburg. Here was a black community of over 300 people living on dugong, turtles and king-fish, and completely removed from the rest of the world. This quiet radio man wandered around the well-laid out village with its store, school and church, and finally measured out the site for the future aerial masts near the Mission housing, sensing at every step that Flynn's dream had a special urgency in it for a place like this isolated community. He sat up late with Flynn and Mr. Wilson to talk about the whole radio and Flying Doctor plan.

They shared news of the Church and the outside world, but their conversation kept on returning to the radio equipment that was under a tarpaulin in the Dodge Buckboard in the Burketown police yard. Traeger revelled in describing the small hand-driven generator and the crystal-controlled transmitter, because Mr. Wilson was keenly aware of the technical difficulties and had himself been experimenting with a self-made telephone between the two Mission houses.

Mr. Wilson, who was to serve with great success on Mornington Island for 22 years, little realised that within 18 months his people would be sending messages to Cloncurry and calling up the Flying Doctor on their own miracle Traeger Transceiver.

Flynn and Traeger got back to Burketown on the Mission boat, picked up the Dodge Buckboard, and were again on the road to Cloncurry, their 'secret mission' successfully completed.

They reached Cloncurry in time for the Melbourne Cup on the first Tuesday in November. Traeger, with his typical boyish delight, rigged up his new aerial mast behind the post office and quickly made contact on his receiving set with the broadcast of the race from Flemington. Reception was crystal clear. People gathered from all quarters. Trivalve, ridden by the veteran jockey Bobby Lewis, won. The people clapped wildly and quickly dispersed for their celebrations at the nearby hotels. Traeger sat on a box and laughed as Flynn bought him a lemon squash. The incident showed Traeger's ready humour, just to be in the fun and for Flynn to meet people. It certainly was a good example of broadcast reception, but Alf was not yet putting his 'real' wireless on public show!

However, the next evening a meeting of Cloncurry citizens and pastoralists from the district was arranged by the Shire Council, and during the afternoon

Traeger had pulled up with the Dodge Buckboard outside the Shire Hall and set up the shortwave telephony set that Harry Kauper had encouraged him to include with the other radio gear. For power Traeger linked it with the 32-volt electric light generator plant that served the shire hall. When the meeting with Flynn concluded in the hall, Traeger had Harry Kauper on the air in Adelaide. Alf invited the Deputy Chairman of the Shire Council to say a word to Kauper who was giving such help in the wireless experiments. He first of all declined very vigorously, but in the end the people who gathered around couldn't get him to stop! It was a practical exhibition of what Flynn had been describing to the people in the hall, and it helped him the next day to make arrangements with the Shire Clerk, Mr. Hargrave, for the setting up of a local Aerial Medical Service Committee.

Traeger, now 32 years old, wearing his customary dark trousers with braces, had really become part of the Queensland Gulf Country and its people on the isolated station properties. He also now had a clear picture of three actual sites where his first radio sets would be installed.

Flynn and he travelled back through Bourke to Cobar and then to Melbourne where they arrived just in time for a widely advertised meeting, and where Traeger caught the train to Adelaide. At home he yarned into the night with his father and his brother Jack, who were eager listeners to his enthusiastic story. His "Take me to Cloncurry" experience had been historically and personally memorable. Traeger had been on the road with his boss for over two months. Sending messages with a hand driven generator. Camping in lonely and solitary places. Talking for long hours. Meeting bush people. Taking turns at the steering wheel of the faithful Dodge Buckboard. Laughing with the Mornington Island crewmen who sailed the *Morning Star*.

By this time Traeger had one compelling urge – to get back to his workshop and carry out additional refinements on the equipment he had been using. His mind was set on producing the compact, inexpensive, and easy-to-operate baby machine of Flynn's dreams. Since he had been at Mornington Island nothing was going to stop him.

CHAPTER SIX

He Put On His Sunday Suit

1928 was a year of big events. On 23rd February Bert Hinkler landed at Darwin on his historic record solo flight from London in his single-engined Avro Avian. Kingsford Smith and Ulm headed their Southern Cross across the Pacific Ocean from America to Australia on 31st May. A fortnight earlier John Flynn's Aerial Medical Service was established in Cloncurry, a bush township in North West Queensland, with Dr. Kenyon St. Vincent Welch and pilot Captain Arthur Affleck making the first emergency medical flight in a single-engine de Havilland 50A aircraft on 17th May.

At the same time, however, there was another worldscale happening taking place in an unpretentious workshop in Adelaide, where an extraordinary pedal wireless contraption was being constructed that was destined also to make headline history. Bert Hinkler, Charles Kingsford-Smith, Arthur Affleck the Flying Doctor pilot and Alfred Traeger – all young men in their mid-thirties – were leading Australia into a twin revolution in the whole field of aeroplanes and bush wireless.

On 20th May 1928 Jean Baird, Secretary at the Australian Inland Mission head office in Sydney, wrote to Traeger saying that Flynn, before taking his holiday overseas, wanted to make a final visit to Cloncurry with a group of interested people to see something of the new Aerial Medical Service and other recent happenings. The suggestion was that Traeger should join the party and travel with the new patrol padre, George Scott.

During the last week of May, Traeger recruited two young assistants from his local Lutheran Church to work with him as radio apprentices and to take charge while he himself was away. Flynn had explained that this second trip to Cloncurry was mainly to enable him to take photographs for promotional work overseas, and to have consultations with the local Flying Doctor Committee.

There were three vehicles in the expedition. John Bicket, a lusty senior school boy from Scots College Sydney, offered to be Flynn's driver in the new Dodge car that was to be the patrol vehicle in Cloncurry. George Towns and Ernest Gollan, special radio friends, with Norman Orr, Flynn's mapping expert, travelled in the second car. Traeger and Rev. George Scott were in the well-seasoned Dodge Buckboard.

They set off from Sydney on 20th June, arriving in Cloncurry on 1st July. Flynn was invited to stay in the home of Mr. P.G. Knyvett, the local magistrate, who was a vital member of the Presbyterian Church Committee and who had initiated the proposal to provide electric light in the church and manse before the new minister arrived. The installation of this 32-volt lighting plant in a small building at the rear of St. Cuthbert's Church was another providential happening in May of that year because, with some modification, it became the first 'powerhouse' for the original base station VJI, which Traeger and Harry Kinzbrunner set up the next year.

On the day after arrival in Cloncurry, the touring party met Dr. St. Vincent Welch and Captain Arthur Affleck at the Post Office Hotel and drove to the aerodrome. Traeger excitedly climbed into the cabin of the rugged biplane with its ambulance stretcher, and with keen interest sat quietly in the seat where the Flying Doctor carried out his work. Dr. Welch had already spoken about the possible tragedy that could happen at any time if, for instance, a mother on a distant cattle station with a desperately ill baby had no chance of calling for medical help. Traeger was silent. "Someday," he mused to himself, "someday we'll even have a wireless set which the doctor can use while flying in the air." Frustrating experiments, however, had to be carried out for nearly five years before this hope was to be fully realised. It was on 31st July 1934 this added miracle took place. Dr. Jock Rossell, on a long-distance flight to Innamincka, became the first doctor in the world to carry out a medical consultation from the air with the nursing sisters at Innamincka Hospital as they battled to save the life of a critically ill patient.

From the Cloncurry airfield, the party went back to St. Cuthbert's Presbyterian Church in Uhr Street where Traeger, Towns, Gollan and the patrol padre George Scott rigged up at the side of the church building the amateur 50-watt wireless set that Alf had brought with him. Traeger Morse-coded a surprise call to Harry Kauper in Adelaide on the 80-metre band. Flynn took a photograph of Traeger in his working clothes as he operated the wireless set. On his trip to Scotland the following year this was one of the important pictures on a lantern slide that Flynn used to illustrate a lecture on 'Radio in Medicine' to the Highlands and Island Medical Service.

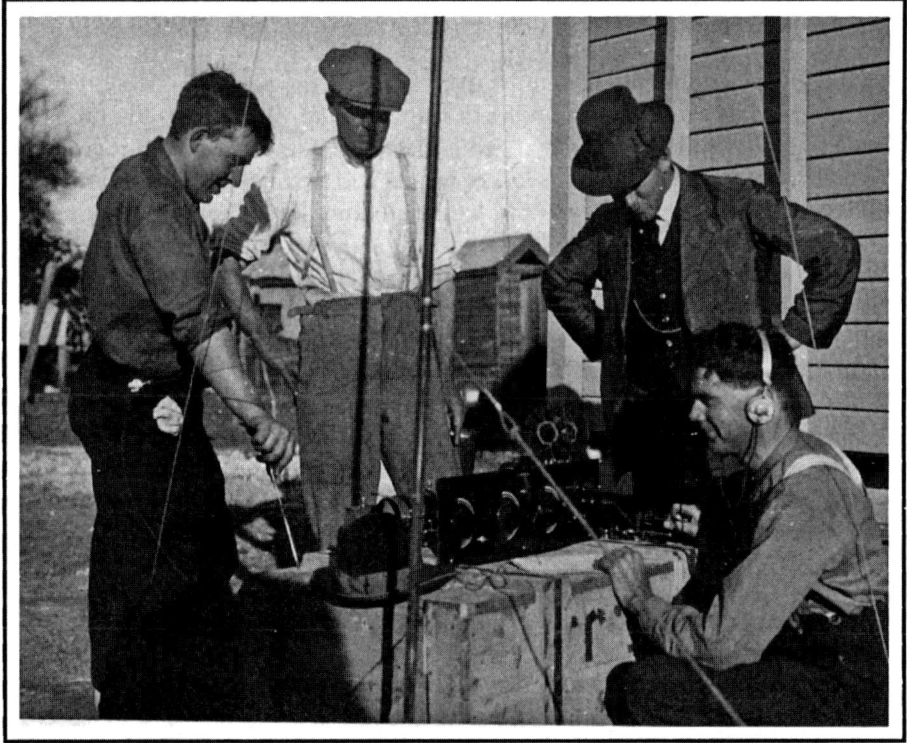

Traeger transmitting a Morse code message on his experimental 50-watt set at the side of the Presbyterian Church, Cloncurry. From left: George Towns, Ernest Gollan, Padre George Scott. (Picture taken by John Flynn, July 1928.)

In Flynn's later report on the 1928 visit to Cloncurry he explained that there has been an attempt to install a temporary 50-watt station in the church to be ready for experimental tests, but after a hurried 'try-out' by the three radio men – Traeger, Towns and Gollan – the stint was abandoned as being impractical at that time.

From Cloncurry Flynn and Bicket set off in the Dodge Tourer on an extended visit to the Northern Territory while Traeger caught the train back to Adelaide. He recalled with smiling good humour an experience he had on the Townsville-Brisbane express. When he entered his sleeper berth there was a lady in his bed! The conductor was at a loss to explain the double booking and transferred the reluctant lady to another carriage. And Alf laughingly said that he had fears all night that at any moment she might return to his cabin to renew her enterprising hopes!

By the end of July he was back in his workshop in Adelaide, which he had now shifted to a nearby bigger building in Cathro Terrace at Carryton. The next five months were probably the most climactic in his whole life. Flynn was leaving Australia on his overseas holiday in six months' time and Traeger's determined resolution was that his boss would see his wireless dream fulfilled before he boarded ship for Cairo and London.

Louise Traeger, the family mother, now in her 57th year, woke Alf at daylight each morning as she packed him off to his workshop with a carefully prepared basket of food for the long hours of work that were now the regular programme. She had grave concerns about his loss of weight and tiredness and longed for each Sunday to come when he joined the family at church and then slept the rest of the day. His father, Johann, coming on to 58 years of age, made a habit of turning up at the workshop by midday to help where he could. But Traeger himself was buoyed up by the task he was facing. He had the quiet, obstinate spirit of his mother. He was going at all costs to get the job done.

He first of all concentrated on the straight-forward radio work in remodelling the receiver and transmitter into the compact and easy-to-operate baby set that Flynn required.

His brother Jack and the two young mechanical assistants got to work putting together the neat cabinet that was to house the combination transceiver unit. They constructed the top of the case as a hinged lid to allow inspection and servicing. The whole cabinet was made of strong pine timber, easily transportable, and painted black.

By this time it was mid-August. Traeger was keeping up to his disciplined schedule, and he now turned to the hand-operated generator that had given such effective results in the trial tests on the road with Flynn during the previous year.

However, Traeger had by now become sensitively aware of the practical problems that would face mothers of the bush homes who would naturally be the main operators of his wireless sets. He knew that it would be an almost impossible task to tap out messages in Morse code and at the same time operate a hand-driven generator.

It was quite a moment in Australian history. Traeger in his dark trousers and braces was sitting on a box near his work bench munching his lunch. It was his birthday, 2nd August 1928. His brother Jack, who later recalled the dramatic incident, described Alf suddenly standing up with a sandwich in his hand and making the forthright declaration that from that moment he was going to forget hand-driven generators. "I am going to buy bicycle pedals," he said. It was the stubborn resolution of his 33rd birthday, in spite of the thinking of Flynn his boss.

Claims have been made that Traeger borrowed the idea of using bicycle pedals for radio transmission from the German Army in World War I. The modern radio researcher Mervyn Eunson categorically dismisses this myth stating – "No valve transmitters existed at the time of World War I and the Germans relied on bulky Telefuncken spark apparatus. These required vast amounts of power, supplied by huge motor-driven alternators which were not portable. The British used similar advanced Marconi spark sets." Eunson also claims that if any pedal-operated radio existed in wartime (1914-1918) it would have been a well-known fact to communication researchers and Traeger would have been saved a lot of trouble!

The miracle pedal generator.

John Flynn reported casually, however, that he had seen a bicycle-mounted dynamo arrangement used in a travelling Pathe picture show but he discountenanced it completely because of its low voltage supply. Mervyn Eunson wastes no words in repeating his definite claim that "it was Traeger's inventive genius, his down-to-earth engineering skills, and his experience in winding electrical armatures which set him apart in Australian history as the solitary individual mastermind behind the creation of the unique pedal wireless generator".

Back in Winton in the previous year Flynn had become convinced that the hand-driven generator was 'the miracle', and he still vehemently retained this conviction. Traeger had therefore shared his drawings with the manager of the Adelaide Foundry, who had moulds and metal castings to house this hand-winding machine, for use on the road in 1927, but it was later discovered that in his tool box he had an optional set of bicycle pedals that he didn't show his boss!

When Traeger had detailed the specifications of the dynamo that he required, he sent the design drawings to George Towns, his radio friend in Sydney. Mr. Reg Cox of the Machinery and Electrical Company in Sydney agreed to construct 12 generator units as an urgent contract. Traeger himself, the skilled engineer, gave personal detailed attention to the driving gears of the pedal generator. Two dozen nickel-plated bicycle pedals were obtained from the Malvern Star Company, the deal being negotiated by Mr. Jack Hale of the Newton McLaren Company in Adelaide.

When Traeger finally assembled his first complete baby transceiver he set it on a table – expertly boxed, control knobs nicely labelled, transportable, easy to operate, ready for all kinds of bush conditions. He then fixed to the floor beneath the table the queer-looking generator with its shining bicycle pedals.

It was late in the day, 11th November 1928. Traeger was tired out. "Victory at last," he said under his breath, "and thank God." Five months previously he has seen the word 'Victory' painted by John Flynn on the side of the Flying Doctor plane in Cloncurry. He wrote a quick note to Flynn – "Come and see the real 'Victory' before you go on your holiday trip."

Flynn caught the train for Adelaide, and turned up at Traeger's workshop. It was 17th November. It was a moment of history. These two extraordinary men meeting one another that day. Traeger with his very shy disposition and his cautious smile simply said, "Well, there it is!"

Flynn was a man not given to physical embraces. But he was not ashamed to show inward emotion. He slowly and earnestly said three words – "Mobs of thanks!" This was Flynn, deeply moved, expressing his flooding gratitude.

"Go home and get into your Sunday suit," Flynn at length continued. "I want to take a very important photograph."

Traeger got out of his working trousers and braces and put on his Sunday suit. And with some embarrassment he posed for the photograph of himself and his pedal wireless 'contraption' – the photograph that is now so historically and universally famous.

In a very real sense the greatest moment of the year 1928 was when Traeger put on his Sunday suit to show his boss, Flynn of the Inland, what the miracle pedal wireless machine really looked like.

"He put on his Sunday suit."

CHAPTER SEVEN

The New Term 'Pedal Wireless'

Flynn caught the train back to Sydney to start packing his bags for his well deserved overseas holiday. He had smilingly farewelled Traeger with two simple and straightforward words. He just looked at him and said, "Carry on". And Traeger knew exactly what John Flynn meant.

There were no written instructions. The trust between these two utterly different characters and their commonly held radio dream seemed to create within them a kind of shared spiritual force that would never allow them to give up whatever happened.

Traeger realised full well that the urgent vision of his boss was to have at least 10 completed baby wireless sets ready for installation in bush homes as soon as humanly possible.

In November 1928 a young man called Harry Kinzbrunner, who had heard about Traeger, came looking for an opportunity to train as a radio mechanic. Three months later Traeger recommended that Kinzbrunner be appointed as his assistant and to accompany him as an unqualified but reliable operator of the mother station that was being planned for Cloncurry.

Traeger also recruited four additional part-time helpers from among his friends in the Bethlehem Church. He was therefore gathering around him a team of reliable and industrious fellow workers who would also join him every Sunday at Church as good, exemplary Lutherans.

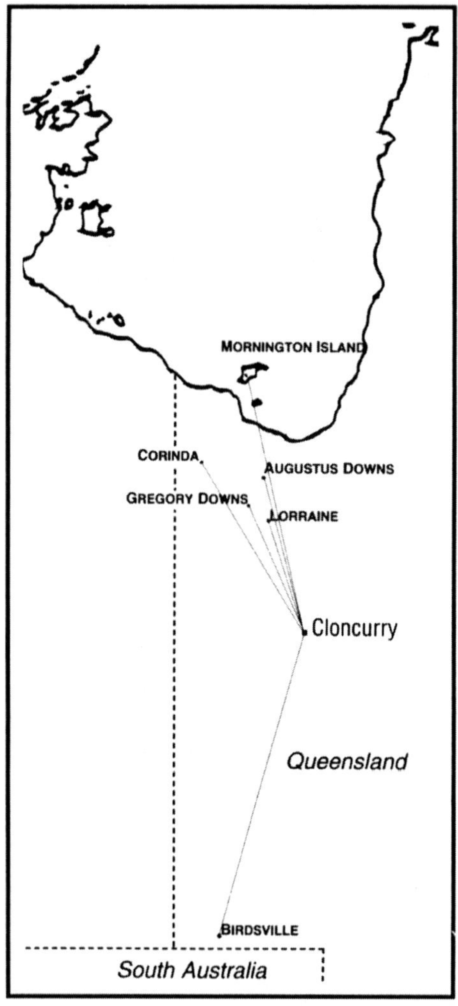

During the period May-November 1929, Traeger established his own designed mother station in Cloncurry and installed his first six baby sets, travelling hundreds of kilometres on bush roads.

The difficult task of machining the gears of the pedal generating machine in their precise ratios was undertaken by the head engineer of Weymouth Motors Ltd, with Traeger standing beside the lathe with a measuring gauge in his hand.

By 10th April Traeger had 10 complete baby sets with pedal generators ready for despatch, as well as the 200-watt mother set for the base-station transmitter that Harry Kauper had helped to assemble and test in his workshop at 5CL Radio Station.

Mr. Jack Hale, of the Adelaide firm of Newton McLaren Ltd, again came forward as Traeger's expert packer, because this total valuable consignment had to be taken by ship from Port Adelaide to Brisbane, by ship again to Townsville, and then by rail to Cloncurry – a complete distance of half-way round the continent. The eight well-labelled and important-looking cases left Port Adelaide on 16th April on its long, six-week journey.

By mid-May Traeger and Kinzbrunner met up with Padre George Scott in Sydney, who was waiting with his Dodge car and 'Gulf Patrol' trailer for the road trip to Cloncurry. The slow and adventurous road journey caused by floods gave Traeger some anxiety about getting to Cloncurry in time to track down what was happening with his precious load of baby sets, but when they finally arrived in Cloncurry on 28th May they were met by Captain Arthur Affleck, the Flying Doctor pilot, at the manse in Uhr Street. "Have you heard anything about the wireless gear?" Traeger blurted out. Affleck replied quite indifferently, "It is all in the church vestry".

The culminating adventure now began. The first priority was the setting up of the mother station in the church vestry and the linking-up operation with the electric light plant in the shed outside. A big crowd of Cloncurry people attended the opening ceremony on 6th June. Traeger called up his special friend Harry Kauper in Adelaide. The people clapped.

Now came the moment about which Traeger had been dreaming when on 18th June he set off with Padre George Scott with No.1 pedal set and the aerial gear safely packed in the Gulf Patrol trailer linked to the parish car.

Harry Kinzbrunner was left in charge of the mother station. Scott and Traeger were headed for a cattle station called Augustus Downs, 300 kilometres northwards on the road to Burketown. They had confirmed their plans with Mr. F.H. Brodie in Cloncurry before leaving because he was the 'Kidman man' for the whole Gulf region and was a collaborator in the John Flynn, Sidney Kidman secret plan that Augustus Downs would be the experimental site for the very first pedal wireless.

Kidman had taken up the important property Augustus Down, in 1878 as a group of holdings of five conjoined pastoral areas. He used the property with its annual rainfall of over 500mm for running big numbers of mixed Hereford cattle, and a section of the area along the Leichhardt River for breeding horses.

Mr. George Rothery, a very capable cattle man, was the manager during the years 1927-1934 when Flynn was starting the Flying Doctor scheme. His wife, Gertrude, was 29 years of age, caring for a baby, Beryl, of six months, with a lively young son, Alan, aged two and a half, also very much in the picture. Ian and Janice later made the complete family of four children. George and Gertrude Rothery were well known and highly respected community people. They owned a black Essex car, and the children were brought up to enjoy tennis parties on the other station properties.

Traeger and Scott arrived at Augustus Downs late in the afternoon of 18th June. The station homestead was a typical bush home on high blocks. Traeger with John Flynn had met the Rothery family two years previously on their special trip to Mornington Island, so he was ready immediately to position the aerial poles and unload the wireless gear on a table in the downstairs section of the homestead.

It was Traeger's first experience of training a lady as a wireless operator. With some embarrassment he sat beside Gertrude Rothery the next morning to guide her hands in using the Morse keyboard. Mrs. Rothery herself was obviously nervous about this entirely new and strange exercise. To her last days at the age of 92 years in a nursing home in North Rockhampton, Gertrude Rothery continued to speak of the whole experience with an alert memory and good humour. In her wheelchair, unable to write herself, she dictated a letter to be forwarded by Leah, the wife of her eldest son, Alan:

Dear Mr. McKay,

I am sending you this letter from my wheelchair to let you know what really happened when Mr. Traeger came to put in the first wireless set in our home at Augustus Downs. Leah is really writing this letter for me because I cannot write any more.

"I get a bit proud because everybody seems to know that I was the person who worked the very first pedal radio." – *Mrs. Gertrude Rothery operating No. 1 pedal wireless installed by Alfred Traeger at Augustus Downs on 19th June 1929. The cabinet was built of wood. The whole set was remodelled in a metal case the following year.*

I get a bit proud because everybody seems to know that I was the person who worked the very first pedal radio when it was fixed up in our home in June 1929. I was 29 years of age and my second baby was only six months old. I was terribly nervous. I pedalled the generator and sent the first telegram in Morse code.

Mr. Traeger was a marvellous man and I will never forget his patience. I was his first pupil and I knew he was shy about ladies. But he was so patient and helpful, and he stayed with us about seven days to make sure that I understood everything. He worked quietly and you would never think he was so clever.

The men couldn't believe the marvellous way he joined up the pipes to make the aerial pole and then pulled it up with wire ropes. The Aboriginal stockmen got a terrible fright when the big pole was halfway up and looked like breaking in the middle, but Mr. Traeger and Mr. Scott knew what they were doing and by midday the tall pole was standing upright with the aerial wires hanging down.

Then Mr. Traeger bolted the black pedal machine on the floor and joined it to the radio case on the table. Following that he worked for a long time connecting up the wires through the roof and out to the aerial pole. He then lifted the lid of the radio case and showed me the valves and the crystal which had to be safeguarded from dust and cleaned with methylated spirits. I watched everything he did and made him brownie cake for smoko.

He slept on the verandah and got up early when my husband made tea in the kitchen. He was amused at the big pieces of meat the stockmen ate for breakfast. He liked my home-made bread, but he had never seen tinned butter before and it used to get very rancid because we had no refrigeration in those days – only a drip safe. He was amazed at the way we used to hang up slabs of beef in our meat house when the men killed a bullock. He didn't like the look of it because it dried out and went very dark in colour. But he liked eggs and tinned meat. Dear Mr. Traeger must have thought we were strange people but he always smiled and went on with his work. He was not a talker but he liked to listen to the men tell yarns at night. Quite often he worked with a carbide lamp at the radio at night, but we had no electric light and that made it difficult. In any case everybody went to bed early.

Mr. Traeger helped me to practise sending the word "Hello" on the Morse key. So when I was ready to work the pedals and send my first message to Harry Kinzbrunner in Cloncurry Mr. Traeger sat beside me and after my 'Hello" he said 'That's great – now go ahead and send the telegram to Mr. Flynn in Sydney". So I sent the first proper telegram on the pedal wireless and I sent it without any mistakes. Later I heard that Harry Kinzbrunner said that I sent 'O Hell' and not 'Hello!' Mr. Traeger on his next visit laughed and was a bit annoyed and explained that it was not possible for me to send it like that. But it was a good joke and I don't mind. I came to enjoy working the pedal wireless and I looked forward to Harry Kinzbrunner's call to me every morning. He was a good man and helped everybody.

Well, that is about all I can say. When the pedal wireless worked so marvellously and we were able to call up the Flying Doctor and even send messages and telegrams, it was the biggest thing that ever happened in my life in the bush. So Mr. Traeger will always be our special friend. The pedal wireless saved our lives.

Yours sincerely,

Gertrude Rothery.

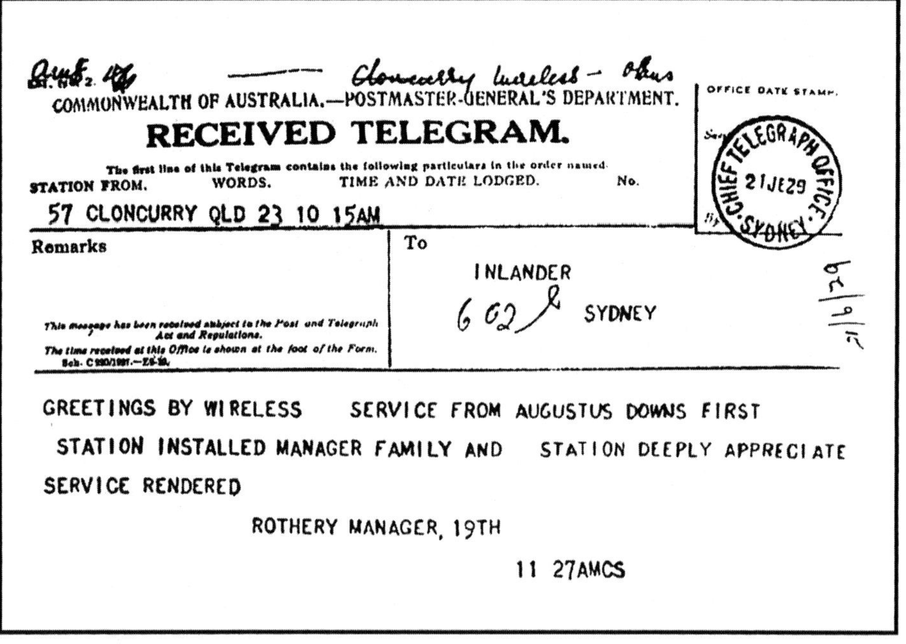

COMMONWEALTH OF AUSTRALIA.—POSTMASTER-GENERAL'S DEPARTMENT.

RECEIVED TELEGRAM.

The first line of this Telegram contains the following particulars in the order named.
STATION FROM. WORDS. TIME AND DATE LODGED. No.

57 CLONCURRY QLD 23 10 15AM

OFFICE DATE STAMP. CHIEF TELEGRAPH OFFICE · SYDNEY · 21JE29

Remarks

This message has been received subject to the Post and Telegraph Act and Regulations.
The time received at this Office is shown at the foot of the Form.

To

INLANDER
602 SYDNEY

GREETINGS BY WIRELESS SERVICE FROM AUGUSTUS DOWNS FIRST STATION INSTALLED MANAGER FAMILY AND STATION DEEPLY APPRECIATE SERVICE RENDERED

ROTHERY MANAGER, 19TH

11 27AMCS

The historic first pedal wireless telegram.

The Augustus Downs pedal wireless and Gertrude Rothery, the pioneering operator, set the pattern. The unit worked with surprising success right from the beginning. Today the property is still linked to the Flying Doctor but now it is by radio telephone and owned by the enterprising Stanbroke Pastoral Company, who from 1963 have transformed the station into a breeding domain for some 18000

Brahman cattle and a training ground for jackeroos and jilleroos from all over Australia.

Augustus Downs therefore has a renowned place in Flying Doctor history and in the social revolution that burst upon the outback on the day when Traeger taught a lady to send messages on a pedal radio. And David and Doreen Dollard, who champion the destiny of Augustus Downs in these later days, proudly display on the main wall of the station office an enlarged colour copy of the original pedal wireless telegram – unique in the world!

During the next five months Traeger and Scott undertook trip by trip from Cloncurry to Lorraine, Gregory Downs, Birdsville, Mornington Island and Corinda installing complete pedal wireless units in each place – a network of baby sets linked up with the mother station in Cloncurry on the 88-metre band – giving a voice to four isolated stations, an outback hospital and an Aboriginal community.

The technical achievement represented a practical working scheme whereby the two modes of communication, Morse code from the baby sets and telephony from the mother station, combined ingeniously to give a new, exciting voice to the silent bush.

During this period of time Traeger wrote revealing letters to his parents ('Mum and Dad') in Adelaide. There was a youthfulness in the pleasure he was experiencing, and a silent pride in seeing the gratitude of family after family. In addition he wrote about the difficulty he was having in darning his socks, washing shirts on the road, the embarrassment he felt in teaching ladies to operate pedal sets, the fun he had on the *Kallantina*, on the hot journey to Mornington Island, when the Captain treated him overgenerously to four tankards of beer, and the amusement he got from the reaction of Aboriginal people who had never seen bicycle pedals in their lives. His dependence on his father also displayed a remarkable relationship, because every fortnight whether on the road or back in Cloncurry he shared his problems and needs with his father, who was regularly despatching material and equipment to him.

The year did not end without its sad happenings. The baby set at Birdsville Hospital failed to function when Sister Maude Gilbert developed acute peritonitis. She had to be conveyed in a station truck to Boulia, and then by police car for the rest of their journey to Cloncurry, a total distance of 640 kilometres by slow and rough roads. Sister Gilbert died in the Cloncurry Hospital two days later on November 2nd and her grave in the local cemetery bears solemn witness to the grim battle that was part of the life of people in the outback when there was no way of calling for medical help.

Traeger was compelled to rush by car to Birdsville in company with the young trainee missionary Jesse Shackleton, who had recently arrived in Cloncurry to assist Padre George Scott. Traeger and Shackleton after their long journey went for a swim in the Diamantina River. Shackleton dived into the water and his body was later rescued with a broken neck. The Birdsville policeman conducted the burial service in the nearby lonely cemetery. Traeger placed a bunch of everlasting daisies on the mound of sand.

Sister Gwen Pearson, Birdsville Hospital – *"Traeger was at last showing he could hold a woman in his arms and cry."*

The sensitive radio man went slowly back to the bush hospital in Birdsville's lonely main street. He spent a day putting the wireless set in full working order again, and also installed a special additional receiver set that had been sent out by the Eddels family of Longreach.

Sister Gwen Pearson was to carry on the complete nursing tasks alone until a companion sister would arrive. She found it difficult to hide her tears. This double tragedy was a deeply hurting grief. Traeger felt the same. Before he set off alone on the return trip to Cloncurry Sister Pearson wept on his shoulder. Alf was at last showing he could hold a woman in his arms and cry. This was a sad week. There were particular reasons why Traeger never forgot it. On arrival in Cloncurry it was a case of giving urgent attention to the mother station and installing the new shortwave band, which was now becoming necessary for effective all-day communication.

In spite of the sorrowful happenings towards the end of the year it had been a history-making 12-month period. A fresh era in bush communication had begun. The new term 'Pedal Wireless' had entered the English language.

CHAPTER EIGHT

Calls From All Over The Bush

The next four years flashed by like a Melbourne Cup Race! The pace was record-breaking. The days of slow, patient and adventuring experiments were over.

Now came the calls for the 'wonder machine' from all corners of the bush, and installations had to be carried out in an area of Australia 20 times larger than the British Isles. This meant for Traeger thousands of kilometres of rough road travel under all sorts of conditions. The wizard radio man therefore became a popular identity on almost every bush track.

In early April 1930 an urgent message from Lorraine Cattle Station of North Queensland was relayed to him in his workshop by Maurie Anderson, who was now the trained operator appointed by the Australian Inland Mission at the Cloncurry Base Station VJI. The message came from the well-respected Burnett family and was carefully transmitted to Cloncurry in Morse code by the third daughter Kathleen who, at 18 years of age, had the outback honour of being the youngest operator in the early pioneering network. Her bed was in the room next to the pedal set that had been installed eight months earlier by Traeger, and one night she was suddenly awakened by the noise of white ants gnawing at the wood of the radio cabinet. This caused some consternation, especially for the children. Kathleen next morning Morse-coded the calamitous news to Maurie Anderson at the Cloncurry mother station!

The pedal set installed at Augustus Downs in June 1929 was encased in a timber cabinet (See Chapter 7). In 1930 Traeger rebuilt this set encasing it in a metal cabinet painted black. This historic set is now housed in John Flynn Place, Cloncurry, with a name plate attached for museum purposes.

Traeger quickly appreciated the problem remembering with some humour that in the previous year he had seen a bedroom door in the Corinda Station homestead almost eaten away by ravaging white ants.

Traeger, with his team, started to work day and night constructing six completely new sheet metal cabinets finished off with black rust-proof paint. The white ant problem also gave him the added urgent reason to arrange immediate visits to all the 1929 baby sets, and upgrade the receivers with an extra valve and build in new 40-metre shortwave transmitters. These vital improvements were designed by Traeger to increase the day-to-day reliability of all the outpost units and to prevent the kind of breakdown that occurred at Birdsville when Sister Gilbert met her tragic death.

Within three weeks he was on the train to Cloncurry with a consignment of radio parts and the six new black metal cases. Etheleen Burnett in retirement remembers that, as a young girl, she was part of the drama when Scott and Traeger turned up at Lorraine to put new parts in their baby set, and she recalls the lively way the family of three girls tried to entertain the reluctant and shy 'radio man' at a bush picnic when his work was done. But he was too busy. He and Scott were on the road again.

But in spite of the fact that Traeger did not take time to enjoy the extended goodwill of this family yet, he fully realised that Egerton and May Burnett with their six children were the typical homemakers of the outback to whom Flynn wanted to bring his mantle of safety. Colleen, the eldest daughter, says it was "better than Christmas Day" when they got their wireless set – the very kind of occasion that called for a rollicking family celebration! The enterprising Ted Flamsteed of modern Lorraine Station has therefore made sure that an important historic relic of the original pedal set equipment used by the Burnett family is preserved with honour in John Flynn Place in Cloncurry.

Traeger and Scott next visited Augustus Downs and then Birdsville, restoring their baby sets in the same way. They discovered that the two new nursing sisters at the Birdsville Hospital were confounded by the 'mysteries of pedal wireless' and that sending Morse-code messages was a long and exhausting task. This whole situation was a critical one for Traeger because the Birdsville baby set was turning out to be a practical life-saver for the local families and the drovers with their mobs of cattle.

Traeger determined to stay for at least four extra days to help Sister Campbell, who was keen to learn morse code "the proper way". This nursing sister was a good pianist and Traeger suggested that she treat the 'dits' and 'dahs' as musical notes. This became her secret in winning the battle. She developed a surprising ability in transmitting messages with the Morse-code sheet propped up in front of the pedal set like a sheet of music!

Following on the death of Sister Gilbert, well-timed negotiations had been opened by the Secretary of the Australian Inland Mission with the P.M.G. Radio Department for the granting of a licence to operate also on the 40-metre shortwave band. This being granted Traeger, with his typical thoroughness, installed not one but two new shortwave transmitters for the Birdsville nursing sisters. Everyone was happy – and Traeger immediately turned his sights to Mornington Island and Corinda – for a further 10 days of heat and flies! Gregory Downs was to be ruled out of the immediate programme because there was no manager on site and the baby set was not being used, so this meant that when the units at Mornington Island and Corinda were replaced Traeger could make urgent tracks back to his workshop.

John Flynn had returned from his overseas trip on 28th February and was amazed at the wireless developments and the pace of the 'skipping around' of Traeger and Scott. How well he also realised that 'skipping around' from Augustus Downs to Birdsville and from Birdsville to Mornington Island was no holiday jaunt, particularly in the prevailing drought conditions and the Australia-wide Depression of the time.

There were other problems, however, which prevented Flynn from getting back to the field. His major concern was to keep the Flying Doctor flying and to continue talking vigorously with the politicians. Traeger was also well aware that the practical side of the whole wireless part of Flynn's Mantle of Safety had now been committed into his hands.

There were also some financial accounting matters that had to be confirmed. Traeger had costed each of the 10 first pedal sets at £33 ($66) and the six improved models of 1930 at £35 ($70) per set. In every instance the A.I.M. Board paid Traeger his complete expenses from their special wireless account, and there was some magic in this because John Flynn was struggling to keep his whole organisation afloat at the same time.

To sell pedal wireless sets on a commercial basis was not allowable within the missionary charter of the A.I.M. This meant that all outpost sets were initially installed as straight-out gifts of good-will. But once the pedal wireless was proved to be efficient and so vital to the well being of bush people practical help and financial donations came from various quarters – 'saints and sinners' alike as Flynn described them. Sir Sidney Kidman promised help from his stations right from the beginning. Other pastoralists did the same. The most gratifying help came from the Country Women's Association. The very first pedal set that Traeger installed in Birdsville in 1929 was a gift from the Queensland C.W.A. Branch at Bundaberg, and in the end there was a series of outpost baby sets that carried plaques with the honoured C.W.A. name upon them.

There were extraordinary rejoicings at Mornington Island when Traeger completed the radio restoration in the Mission house. Rev. R.H. Wilson, the Superintendent, arranged with the Aboriginal people with their crowding children to gather at the pier as the Mission lugger pulled away with Traeger waving lustily. Mr. Wilson in a letter to John Flynn said, "The Traeger wireless made us part of the world".

George Johnstone, the big-framed manager of Corinda cattle station, gave Traeger a crushing handshake when he turned up to renovate their machine. When the measles epidemic had struck the Aboriginal camp at Turn Off Lagoon Johnstone had to make contact with the Flying Doctor every week, but the main delight of this cricket enthusiast was that, on the day Traeger added the extra valve to the receiver of the pedal set, he was able to hear the broadcast of Bradman making 354 runs in the Test at Leeds in England!

Back at Cloncurry four new pedal sets with aerial masts were waiting for Traeger's next urgent trip.

Hermannsburg was first. To see Pastor Albrecht again would be to keep alive their warm bonds of friendship, and Traeger whistled as he packed the wireless gear in the Dodge Buckboard.

On this trip to the Northern Territory George Scott wanted first of all to make a pastoral call to the nursing sisters at Maranboy A.I.M. Hospital. This proved to be an extended visit because in the end the Dodge Buckboard was parked at Maranboy while George Scott arranged for a group to join him in a rail trip to Darwin.

Traeger and Scott eventually got on the road to Alice Springs. George Scott, who had contracted a dose of influenza, was detained for two days in the A.I.M. Hospital and Traeger drove on alone to Hermannsburg. It was like a homecoming. Young Edwin Pareroultja, now aged 11 years, rushed out to meet him. Pastor Albrecht later wrote a letter: "Never in my life shall I forget what he (Traeger) meant to me. He was the man who brought me a wonderful comfort and feeling of relief because we knew we were not cut off any longer and we had a new sense of safety."

When the new pedal set was installed Traeger became involved with the crowd of people with cars who had come to Hermannsburg and Palm Valley for the so-called Reso Rally. One of their members suffered a massive heart attack and died. Rev. George Scott had by this time recovered from his influenza attack and had joined Traeger at Hermannsburg. The Resonians gathered around in amazement as Traeger sent and received urgent radio messages to and from the bereaved family in Melbourne. The body was wrapped in a blanket and sewn up in white canvas for air despatch to Melbourne. Rev. George Scott held a service in the Hermannsburg Mission Chapel. Traeger's pedal wireless was again the miracle machine.

Before leaving Hermannsburg the old dust-ridden radio set and Edison batteries of the 1926 experiment were loaded into the Dodge Buckboard. The same was done in Alice Springs at the original mother station. Traeger and Scott travelled through Arltunga, Love's Creek, The Pinnacles and The Plenty River.

The original transmitter station VJI in Cloncurry was built by Traeger in his Adelaide workshop and installed in the vestry of the Presbyterian Church, Cloncurry, in June 1929. Improvements were made in successive years.

Bulldust. Flies. Kangaroos. Roadside camps at night. They crossed the Northern Territory border into Urandangie and home to Cloncurry. Traeger had a haircut and slept for a day!

The next round-up was another extraordinary experience – Bedourie, Innamincka, Borroloola – a bush hotel, a bush hospital and bush police station! The George Gaffney family at the Bedourie Hotel closed the bar so that Padre Scott could hold a celebratory Church service after the pedal set was installed. At Innamincka, after battling over the sandhills, Traeger patiently sat with Sister Burchill and helped her to call up Dr. Spalding, the new Flying Doctor in Cloncurry. She talked about it all her life!

Pointing the Dodge car towards Borroloola was like setting out for another world, a winding, slow bush road of over 1600 kilometres.

On 11th August Flynn received a telegram in Sydney:

"Congratulations and sincere regards from Borroloola folk on the inauguration of the wireless service. We consider yours is the first footstep on the sand of times into a new era."

Borroloola was an isolated village of some 60 people on the McArthur River, 80 kilometres inland from the Gulf of Carpentaria. Since 1893 the main building in the lonely single street was a police house. Commissioner Stretton in Darwin was so gratified when Traeger installed the pedal wireless in the policeman's family home that he forwarded an immediate cheque and ordered a further baby set for Anthony Lagoon. Flynn received a sudden ominous complaint from Amalgamated Wireless of Australia that the A.I.M. organisation was exceeding legal bounds by commercially selling wireless equipment. A semi-humorous legal situation confronted Flynn but his friendship with Ernest Fisk of A.W.A. won the day and Traeger went off blithely to help another Northern Territory policeman without worrying about commercial deals.

Returning to Cloncurry Traeger spent a valuable three weeks with Mr. Maurice Bernard Anderson, who had taken over the control of the Base Station. Maurie was to become a never-to-be forgotten voice on the Cloncurry radio network for the next nine years. Kinzbrunner went back into civilian life when his year of pioneering work was over at the mother station and Anderson, later joined by another well-trained radio operator, Vernon Kerr, initiated professional management for the next critical phase of the quickly developing Cloncurry network. Anderson introduced the radio technique that brought efficiency and a popular simplicity into the whole scheme, and his technical experience meant that Traeger now had an expert to carry out modifications and improvements as they became necessary.

For the next three weeks Traeger and Anderson worked together in the vestry of the Presbyterian church rebuilding the whole transmitter equipment and discussing plans for the immediate search for another more suitable property where the base station could be established.

A central figure in the pedal radio story during this pioneering period was Mr. Eric Hatswell, who became postmaster in Cloncurry in October 1928, and held this position for eight years. Hatswell and Traeger developed an important and close kinship, Traeger often spending after-work hours at the Hatswell home behind the post office, discussing the day-to-day telegraphic activities that were their common concern. Eric Hatswell was an experienced telegraphist and took immediate interest in the pedal radio telegrams that came into his hand for onward transmission from the mother station in the vestry of the Presbyterian church. These pedal radio telegrams were first delivered by Kinzbrunner on foot and later by Vernon Kerr on a bicycle. To Eric Hatswell goes the honour of telegraphing to 'Inlander' Sydney Mrs. Rothery's first telegram. His grandchildren prize the historic copy they have of this first-in-the-world pedal radiogram.

This friendly partnership between the Cloncurry Post Office and the A.I.M. mother station was a notable reason for the professional efficiency and promptness that became an outstanding feature when the pedal radio telegrams increased in substantial numbers each day. It became the same kind of warm-hearted relationship that existed between the Ambulance people and the Flying Doctor. Eric Hatswell was also the moving spirit, once his radio branch gave final approval for non-licensed people to operate pedal sets, in negotiating an official scheme whereby the Australian Inland Mission received a percentage of financial return for each pedal radio telegram.

This arrangement, as Flynn admitted, was applauded and welcomed on all sides because every home where a pedal wireless had been installed now became a virtual telegraphic office.

Traeger went home to Adelaide with one recurring unsolved difficulty on his mind. He and Maurie Anderson had listened-in to the sister from Innamincka and the policeman from Borroloola on their pedal sets. Sending long messages in Morse code was a distressing problem. Traeger was now back in his workshop puzzling out some kind of automatic mechanism that would solve this problem for everybody.

CHAPTER NINE

Taking The Tears Out Of Morse Code

He carefully packed it in a case and caught the train for Sydney. Traeger couldn't help chuckling to himself. The problem of sending Morse-code messages would never be the same again. Even a child could now be an expert.

Flynn had suggested that Traeger bring his new machine to Sydney for the 1931 March meeting of the Executive Committee of the A.I.M. Board. After he unpacked the case and placed the unusual contraption on the boardroom table, he sat down and quietly grinned at the obvious look of surprise on the face of Mr. David Sneddon, the Chairman.

The machine had the outward appearance of a typewriter. The members of the Executive Committee stood around as Traeger explained how it operated. It was his innovative and specially designed automatic Morse keyboard to help inland people to send messages on their baby sets without having to face the difficult task of learning Morse code.

The keys were those of a regular typewriter with some added ones to meet the needs of certain necessary radio signs. These keys were attached to metal arms on the sides of which the 'dits' and 'dahs' were cut in the form of small depressions so that when a particular key was pressed down a roller would follow these small indentations of dots and dashes and register the relevant alphabetical letter[1].

---

1 The technical details of the operation of the automatic Morse keyboard with illustrative pictures are given in the Appendix.

Traeger invented the ingenious automatic Morse keyboard in 1931, and even after telephony was introduced in 1935, this machine was used as an emergency stand-by until 1939.

The Committee unanimously approved that Traeger proceed immediately to produce 20 units for distribution to bush people and to follow up with additional production as necessary.

With a sense of contented satisfaction Traeger went back to Adelaide. However, as he mused in the train, there was another ardent secret plan in his mind. He would send the very first automatic Morse keyboard to the nursing sisters at Birdsville. And this he eventually did. Traeger cherished an unforgettable memory of the lonely December day of the previous year when Sister Pearson had wept in his arms as they shared together the tragedy of the deaths of Sister Gilbert and Jesse Shackleton.

The world didn't know it, but the very first automatic Morse keyboard actually went by urgent rail in January 1932 to Marree and then by carrier truck up the Birdsville Track. The two Birdsville sisters got the surprise of their life.

A few years later a robust bush romance developed between another nursing sister at Birdsville and the popular man who ran the transport trucks from Marree to Birdsville. Their love-making was carried out in the evenings by Morse code.

Maurie Anderson, base operator from Cloncurry, overseeing the erection of the aerial pole for the pedal wireless at the Birdsville Hospital. The Traeger radio masts became a popular symbol along the outback tracks.

A real part of their eventual marriage bliss was born out of an automatic Morse keyboard!

On his return to Adelaide from the Sydney meeting Traeger had geared up his team of helpers in his own workshop and at Newton McLarens for the production of 20 Morse-code machines as well as a continuing series of pedal sets. The so-called "Traeger Transceiver" enterprise was taking its first real public shape.

At the same time out at Cloncurry, scores of bush telegrams were being transmitted month by month as well as medical calls to the Flying Doctor. A mystical kind of 'togetherness' was developing in the bush community every time Maurie Anderson's drawling voice was heard calling up his widespread pedal-radio family.

The author Roger McDonald aptly refers to this new 'contact' that outback people were coming to experience. He quotes: "Radio (became) the great living symbol of the Flying Doctor Service – it stood for the human qualities of contact, connection, consultation and comfort[2]."

By mid April 1931 Traeger was planning his next field trip. Four new pedal sets had been railed to Cloncurry where also the replacement set for Gregory Downs was in store, while the task of installing a new unit at Betoota, halfway between Birdsville and Windorah, was an unknown venture to be faced.

2 *Australian Flying Doctors* (Richard Woldendorp and Roger McDonald, 1994).

In early April Alf had consigned by rail and road via Marree the two cases of equipment for Betoota to Harry Afford at the Birdsville Hotel. He had come to establish an intriguing relationship with the Birdsville publican and the two Gaffney sons, and had entered into an unusual arrangement for them to operate an auxiliary pedal set as an unofficial standby for the A.I.M. Hospital. This plan worked exceptionally well, and it provided a fortunate channel for help when the difficult transport problem of the Betoota equipment had to be arranged. Harry Afford persuaded a special friend, Mr. Charlie Page, to transport the two cases and aerial poles to Durrie cattle station, where the bookkeeper agreed to take the precious load in his station truck the further 50 kilometres in return for a dozen bottles of beer from the Betoota publican!

Traeger back in Adelaide was making preparations for an unforgettable escapade. In the well-seasoned Dodge Buckboard he was determined to drive by himself on one of the roughest tracks in Australia – a 1500-kilometre journey to Betoota via Broken Hill, Innamincka and the sandhill country – so that the isolated people of the Haddon Corner area could have a pedal set.

He strapped to the side of the faithful vehicle the same camel water canteen that he and John Flynn had used five years previously on their Alice Springs adventures. He packed a tuckerbox and swag, a tin of engine oil and four cases of petrol. Also two coils of coir matting for the sandhills and a steel cabinet of tools. But no wireless! For once in his life Traeger felt that he was compelled not to carry valuable wireless gear because of the terrible road conditions.

Johann and Louise Traeger waved and said a prayer as their son set off on this unknown journey. When he finally struggled up the mailman's track from Tibooburra to Innamincka he still had ahead of him over 400 kilometres of sandhills and stones.

For 16 days after he left Innamincka nobody knew where he was! His father wired Cloncurry for news. Maurie Anderson explained that there were no pedal sets in that part of the country. The radio man was lost!

On the 17th day, however, Traeger pulled up outside the Betoota Hotel – tousled hair, sunburnt, and a soiled shirt with no buttons. Mrs. Rumble, the notorious big-bodied lady of the Betoota Hotel, said, "You're mad coming up that bloody track". Traeger had been bogged in the sand at King's Lookout for three days and had broken two springs bumping over rocks south of Cordillo Downs. Traeger smiled ruefully. He slept for an hour on the hotel verandah, but by the end of the day he had two cases of radio equipment unpacked and the aerial poles joined. Early next morning Mr. Sinclair and three stockmen from the nearby Mt. Leonard station turned up in their three-tonne truck loaded with four lengths of mulga timber to serve as guy posts for the aerial mast, a roll of fencing wire, and shovels and crowbars. The men controlled the guy ropes as Traeger used the Dodge Buckboard to pull the aerial mast into position. The pedal set was on the air by late morning. Traeger's first call was to the Cloncurry mother station with a telegram to his father. The news spread that Traeger was still alive! Traeger himself was amused because he had taken the whole incident as a natural course of events in the bush – and Flynn's old Buckboard had done its usual job!

It was the same week of June 1931 that Hudson Fysh was in the midst of critical negotiations leading up to the historic Qantas contract for the England-Australia Mail and Passenger Air Route, Captain Tapp having just completed the first experimental run a fortnight before.

It was the week when John Flynn went to Brisbane to see Premier Forgan Smith to get support for the expansion of the Aerial Medical Service at the forthcoming Premiers' Conference.

It was the week when Dr. George Simpson, Flynn's great offsider, wrote an important letter to the Board of the Australian Inland Mission offering to go to Cloncurry at the end of the month to look into the serious financial situation facing the Aerial Medical Service.

It was the week when 29-year-old Allan Vickers, the Flying Doctor in Cloncurry, took popular Lilias Whitman, daughter of the local chemist, to the open-air picture show when a quick romance started, followed later by a joyful marriage that made Vickers a Cloncurryite forever, and a life-long influence on the wireless and medical developments within the whole Flying Doctor movement.

It was the week when Traeger got the Betoota baby set on the air and was ready to start off again in the battered Dodge Buckboard towards Birdsville and Cloncurry. Sisters Campbell and Fanshawe at the A.I.M. Hospital gave him a great welcome as he placed new valves in their wireless set and explained that someday they may receive an automatic Morse keyboard! They made him stay an extra day so that they could wash and mend his shirts. At Bedourie more wireless work. He got to Cloncurry in the third week of June. There was a letter from his mother – "I get worried, you should not travel so much by yourself on those rough trips. May the Lord always protect you". His mother's letter seemed to throw Traeger into a state of contemplation. He was now 35 years of age. His last birthday had been at Bedourie. His 36th celebration would be on the road somewhere in the Northern Territory. His mother never forgot, but she could never reach him on the day. He sat on the verandah of the Cloncurry church and wrote in reply to her latest letter: "Yes, Mum, God has been my protection. I don't talk about this to people but God has been behind everything I have done."

The year 1931 was showing up certain Traeger qualities of character that were not commonly known. After his harrowing experiences on the road to Betoota he sent home for his old steel guitar, and although it fared badly in the heat it became a lively companion as he strummed songs and hymns in his solitary camps at night. "What is the world coming to?" he asked in a home letter when he explained that he was even taking on the organ at the church services at St. Cuthbert's.

In Cloncurry one of the urgent priorities was to plan with Maurie Anderson for the setting up of a new mother station. Anderson, who was now Secretary of the local Aerial Medical Advisory Committee, had initiated a proposal to transfer a small, disused, country schoolhouse to a site on the road to the Cloncurry Hospital as the new headquarters for VJI. This important task was timed to take place after Traeger had completed his round-up of installations of pedal sets at Gregory Downs, Anthony Lagoon, Rockhampton Downs and Iffley, by which time also the Shire Council would have introduced electric power in the town.

Traeger was now packing the trusty Dodge Buckboard for its final marathon journey. He had developed an affection for Flynn's old vehicle and knew all its mechanical foibles. However, age and hard work had taken its toll. As Alf took the wheel he knew that this would be the last radio round-up that this faithful bush chariot could face[3].

With a load of four pedal sets in addition to aerial poles and rolls of guy wire, the first sortie was to Gregory Downs, Lawn Hill and then into the Northern Territory – Anthony Lagoon, Borroloola and Rockhampton Downs.

The new Cloncurry padre, Bill Dorin, and his wife caught up with Traeger at Camooweal in their parish car. Alf wrote a lighthearted letter to his mother and father about this trip. He was retracing former tracks and his wireless work was among old friends, so he was able to be a guide and helper to the new padre. In the evenings he tried to teach Bill Dorin the skills of sending Morse code. This exercise proved laughably unsuccessful. Mrs Dorin had seen Alf kill a large black snake in their roadside camp the first day, and from that moment she vehemently refused to sleep in her swag on the ground. She propped herself up in the car every night. She got little sleep on the whole trip.

After completing the updating work on the pedal wireless in the Borroloola police house Traeger left Dorin to carry on with his pastoral duties among the people, and in the Dodge Buckboard he set off for Anthony Lagoon. It was Sunday night. He pulled up on the roadside and lit his camp fire. As usual he set up his radio and tuned in to the A.B.C. "I couldn't believe it," he said in his next letter home. "The church service from Bethlehem was on the air. I joined in the hymns with my steel guitar. Pastor Janzow preached a wonderful sermon. In the distant darkness I had a special feeling. I was proud of Bethlehem Church. But the men's choir need to do a lot more practice!"

It was at Anthony Lagoon police station that Traeger made first contact by pedal radio with Rev. Harold Shepherdson, the Methodist Missioner at Millingimbi Aboriginal community. Mr. Shepherdson had taken delivery, while on holiday in Adelaide, of baby sets for Goulburn Island and Millingimbi in faraway Arnhem Land. 'Sheppy' became the champion Morse-code operator on the Cloncurry network. He established a typically warm and important relationship with the A.I.M. staff in Cloncurry, particularly with daily weather reports and emergency information at the time of the murders at Caledon Bay[4].

After completion of the installations in the Northern Territory Rev. Bill Dorin took Traeger in the patrol car loaded with the fifth baby set to Iffley cattle station, south of Normanton in Queensland. Mr. Ernie Camp of Iffley became a central

3 In October 1933 the Dodge Buckboard was sold to Mr. Thomas who operated the pedal wireless at Corinda Cattle Station. Details of the vehicle are given in the Appendix.

4 Copy of telegram from Methodist Overseas Mission in the Appendix.

point of communication on the stock route between Normanton and the Julia Creek railhead, and on each anniversary of Traeger's installation of the baby set, sent a telegram of appreciation to John Flynn from the Flinders River District[5].

At the completion of the year's work there were 20 pedal wireless outstations in daily contact with the mother base operating on two frequencies – 148 metres and 40 metres. In addition Maurie Anderson, flying with Dr. Allan Vickers to Mornington Island, had been experimenting with some success with an adapted baby set for use in the air. Morse communication to and from Cloncurry while travelling over the Gulf waters was loud and clear, but there were further experiments ahead to reach the standard where it was adequate for Flying Doctor consultation[6].

1931 had been a difficult year. "I'm coming home for a spell," Traeger wrote to his parents. He broke the rail journey to spend a day in Toowoomba with Dan and Ted Reimas. In Sydney he and John Flynn went on a ferry to see the almost completed Harbour Bridge. He bought a new pair of trousers and two shirts. He arrived in Adelaide in time for Christmas.

5 Copy of Iffley telegram in the Appendix.

6 The first successful air-to-ground contact for medical purposes by a Flying Doctor was made by Dr. J. McF. Rossell on 31st July 1934 en route to Innamincka.

CHAPTER TEN

Ion Idriess Writes A Book

Few people knew the rigors of outback life better than Ion Idriess. From the age of 19 years he had carried his swag from job to job in the bush areas – prospecting, shearing, buffalo shooting, droving, and at Gallipoli he had narrowly escaped with serious shrapnel wounds.

In 1931 Idriess published *Lasseter's Last Ride*, the baffling story about the search for the mysterious reef of gold out beyond Ayers Rock in Central Australia that ended in Harry Lasseter's tragic death. Idriess met Traeger in Alice Springs returning from Hermannsburg in late 1930. At that time the dramatic story of Lasseter's search for this fabulous reef of gold was the common topic everywhere, and the new baby set that Traeger had just installed for Pastor Albrecht at Hermannsburg was to provide the urgent communication that saved the lives of three people in the fated expedition.

Traeger later back home in Adelaide bought a copy of *Lasseter's Last Ride*, and he and his father vied with one another in being the first to read it. Traeger naturally felt that he had a personal involvement with the Lasseter escapade through the baby wireless at Hermannsburg. He read the book late into the night because he was one of the few people who had heard from Idriess in Alice Springs in 1930 about the other book he was writing – the story of John Flynn and the Australian Inland Mission.

So it happened that Traeger came to mark the 13th May 1932 as one of the unforgettable days of his life. He possessed some strong political ideas about the

The complete equipment (without aerials) of Traeger's updated baby set (1932-33). The fulfillment of the first phase of Rev. John Flynn's dream about breaking the silence of the bush. "We're on the way," he said. "Alf will soon have everyone on telephony!"

notorious Premier of N.S.W. Jack Lang, and sitting at his workbench reading the *Adelaide Advertiser* of that day, he called out to his workmates "Hey, they've sacked him!". To Traeger this was a very righteous happening, and he wasted no words in saying so. However, an hour later came another shattering event that made Traeger forget all about N.S.W. politics. A letter with an accompanying parcel turned up in the mail. It was Jean Baird's last letter. As Secretary of the Australian Inland Mission she had written countless notes to Traeger – some of the most important communications he had ever received about radio experiments, field programmes, and payment of his salary and expenses each month. Now she was Jean Baird no longer. She and John Flynn had fallen in love and had been married in Sydney six days previously on 7th May. Traeger was completely abashed. He couldn't believe what he was reading. "The old boss has got married," he muttered to himself. Jean Baird had joyfully signed her letter as Jean Flynn.

But that was not all. Traeger slowly opened the accompanying package that came with the letter. He gazed in amazement. It was an autographed book from Ion Idriess. Traeger stood holding in his hand a free publisher's copy of *Flynn of The Inland.*

Traeger had been intrigued by the fact that Idriess had made special friendships with the Gaffney family at the Bedourie Hotel north of Birdsville, and had stayed with them a whole week while gathering material about the work of the A.I.M. He had also used their pedal wireless to send messages to Angus and Robertson, his publishers in Sydney, and George Gaffney the publican in his day-to-day conversation had referred to Flynn as *Flynn of the Inland,* the title that Idriess eventually used for his book.

The Traeger parents could not believe the sense of excitement displayed by their radio son. "Read the first three chapters," he said, "that's why I am in this thing – I have never been able to explain it properly." He himself had no concerns about self-glory. Nor did he worry about the incorrect technical radio details in the Idriess story. It was the overall picture that fascinated him.

Idriess had written some of his rough pencilled notes in the train as he travelled from Oodnadatta to Quorn, and in these scribbled jottings he had uncovered his on-the-spot feelings about the meaning of radio in the lives of bush people. He referred to what he called "the first accessible means of communication that came the way of men and women in the Never Never country, and the change it brought" – daily news of home and overseas markets, of weather conditions everywhere, of movements of stock and mail, and of neighbours up and down the distant tracks. In addition to these comments Idriess emphasised in a new way that each pedal wireless in the outback was a "messenger of hope and healing", and that the feeling of "contact" with a Flying Doctor had behind it something mystical. He called it "a great spiritual power[7]".

Traeger scratched his head as he read what Idriess was saying. At that time there were only just over 20 pedal sets in operation, but already a radical social

7 *Flynn of the Inland* (Idriess) Chapters 26-28.

change was sweeping across the distances of the inland, and Idriess was telling the world about it. And there was something in Traeger's boyish smile that showed that he believed that, after all, his mad trip up the Betoota track had been worthwhile.

The period 1932-33 was a rounding-off era in Traeger's field work, five weeks of which, in the middle of 1932, was spent on the road with Rev. Kingsley Partridge, who had returned to his old patrol in Central Australia the previous year.

Traeger met up with Partridge on 31st July 1932. He had packed three cases of wireless equipment on the Oodnadatta train and off-loaded at Farina where Tom McCabe the Innamincka mailman was waiting with Kingsley Partridge.

Partridge, a friendly 40-year-old bachelor, had never been in the Innamincka and Borroloola regions before, so during the next five weeks Traeger and he cemented a new warm friendship, and were quickly exchanging Christian names, which was a fresh procedure for Traeger who did not have this privilege with Scott or Dorin up in the Cloncurry ventures. Although some 10 years later Partridge adopted the name of 'Skipper', Traeger had such an affection for the man that he declined to change the name by which the Padre had introduced himself at Farina the day they first teamed up together. They were 'Kingsley' and 'Alf' to one another for the rest of their lives.

The planned purpose of this five-week trip together was to service and upgrade the previously installed sets at Innamincka, Betoota, Birdsville, Hermannsburg, Rockhampton Downs, Anthony Lagoon and Borroloola, and to install new sets at Diamantina Lakes, Clifton Hills and Victoria River Downs.

Partridge the bushman and Traeger the radio man joined forces on the road together in 1932 when people everywhere were battling against the agonies of the widespread Depression. In their visits to the outback areas they came face to face with travellers looking for work, and with families in the midst of financial distress. This made Maurie Anderson, the base station operator, describe their journeys as 'errands of love and mercy', meeting human needs as well as radio needs. Traeger also referred to the five-week trip with Partridge as a 'sentimental journey', because in place after place his emotions were stirred by the sense of relief and assurance expressed by people just to be part of the radio-network family.

Partridge gradually came to appreciate the place that pedal wireless was taking in the whole social fabric of bush life, and at the end of 1932 he and Traeger began to discuss the possibility of a specially designed mobile pedal set that could be carried in his Dodge car and enable him to communicate direct to the Cloncurry mother station from the roadside. John Flynn enthusiastically recommended to the A.I.M. Board that approval be given to Traeger to design and construct a compact, mobile, pedal-operated transceiver for the use of padres on the road.

Partridge a year later became the pioneer operator of Traeger's twin-boxed mobile set, which was specially constructed so that it could even be carried by camel, horse or truck. There is an historic picture of this original portable transceiver. In 1934 the Centralian Film Production Company sponsored by the enterprising McDonagh sisters was photographing scenes near Haast Bluff at the far end of the McDonnell Ranges west of Alice Springs. They engaged two Aboriginal people, a father and a young son, to participate in a staged act with Partridge showing the operation of his new portable pedal set. The film company presented the picture to the Australian Inland Mission for reproduction with other scenes in a specially designed promotional brochure. Traeger, with his quiet smile, always spoke of this picture with natural disapproval because, as he said, it was neither typical of Kingsley Partridge nor of the Aboriginal man and his boy. The historic fact remained, however, that it was an authentic picture of the first portable pedal set invented and produced by Traeger[8].

In spite of the difficulties of the Depression period, Traeger always referred to his 1932 field-work with Kingsley Partridge as being one of his best memories. To see his long-standing friends at Hermannsburg 'was like coming home', and in radio terms he was always anxious to make Pastor Albrecht his special bush experimenter with any new equipment. In April the next year it was therefore with Albrecht sitting beside him that Traeger carried out his first successful telephony experiment on a baby set. This caused as much excitement as did the first Morse-code message sent four years previously. And Partridge smoked his pipe with gleeful pleasure to see all this happening.

Traeger had also become closely attached to the Hemming family in the police house at Borroloola, to Victor Hall at Anthony Lagoon, and particularly to the George Easey family at Rockhampton Downs. The pedal sets in the homes of these grateful people were not just technical machines. They became visible symbols of a trusted and refreshing relationship. The pedal radio operators were fast becoming a warm-hearted family of scattered people.

The rewarding features of the 1932 field-work were the installations of new pedal sets at Diamantina Lakes for the Harry McCullough family, at Clifton Hills for Norman Gurr and his wife and children, and at the A.I.M. Hospital at Victoria River Downs for the nursing sisters Grace Francis and Elizabeth Hurley. The presence of a pedal wireless in these homes seemed to forge friendships that became life-long. The McCullough family took Traeger to a dinner party with other Kidman friends every time they went to Adelaide. Traeger also formed an extraordinary kinship with the Gurrs of Clifton Hills. Norman Gurr became a bush champion of the A.I.M. and ended his life in the Old Timers' Homes in Alice Springs claiming that it was Alfred Traeger who brought new life into their home on the Birdsville Track.

But with his intensely reserved character Traeger frequently laughed at himself about his instinctive uneasiness in the presence of women. In later life he quite freely admitted that he 'got flustered' when helping nursing sisters to operate a pedal generator and at the same time transmit a message in Morse code. But as he put it 'he couldn't duck the job', and by the time he reached

8 A description of Traeger's original mobile transceivers is given in the Appendix.

Victoria River Downs to meet the two specially chosen nurses he whispered to Partridge, "Mum wouldn't believe it but this is my 10th A.I.M. nursing sister!.

When he got to Victoria River Downs during the last week of August 1932 he soon discovered that Grace Francis could tell him fascinating stories about her grim pioneering work at Birdsville in 1923 with Sister Boyd, before the days of pedal wireless and flying doctors. Traeger found himself sitting up late with the nurses excitedly sharing news of the up-to-date doings in the Birdsville Corner. This made Victoria River Downs an unforgettable experience, and Traeger looked upon it as the consummating field happening of the year, particularly as this hospital was different from the other Flynn experiments because it was an annexe to a cattle station homestead. This made it a unique outpost in the Northern Territory, and Traeger added a new frequency to the transmitter so that the sisters could make contact with the Government radio station at Wave Hill as well as with the A.I.M. mother station in Cloncurry. Partridge also made the Victoria River Downs occasion a significant one in his growing practical experience because he supervised the erection of the 20-metre radio mast by himself, and held a service of blessing to mark the end of the 1932 programme of wireless work in the field.

On 5th September Traeger caught a plane at Newcastle Waters and spent the next month in Cloncurry with Maurie Anderson. These two radio enthusiasts sat

The key people behind the scene. Ethel Hooker, Vernon Kerr and Maurie Anderson kept the mother station open for pedal radio traffic each day. In 1932 the original Flying Doctor base was transferred from the Presbyterian church to an unused schoolhouse that was set up on this site on the main Cloncurry Road.

together in the mother station day after day. In addition to their planning of the permanent frequencies for the long-term efficiency of VJI, their discussions revolved around the personalities and needs of the diverse company of people who made up the family of pedal radio operators. There were now about 25 widely separated outposts – each representing groups of men and women and children previously cut off completely from the rest of the world. Rev. R.H. Wilson of Mornington Island, in his second letter to the Australian Inland Mission office in 1932, expressed the common sentiment of scores of people when he said, "We are unable to express properly what it means to hear Maurie Anderson's voice calling from the mother station each morning – and to be in contact with the Flying Doctor – the whole thing has given us a new peace of mind".

However, both Anderson and Traeger had their hopes centred on upgrading the pedal sets to the stage where the faithful pioneering Morse code would be replaced by first-rate voice telephony. This was to be their dream in the coming two years.

Meantime Traeger was home again in his workshop in Adelaide. His surprising discovery was that a second printing of the popular book *Flynn of The Inland* by Ion Idriess was already on the market, and it was common talk among his friends. Traeger bought a copy of the new edition and presented it to Pastor Janzow at Bethlehem Church as a Christmas gift.

CHAPTER ELEVEN

Then Came The 'Galah Session'

Applause did not come from everywhere. High-ranking officials in the Post Master General's Department continued to have their doubts about pedal wireless being the long-range solution to the communication problem in the outback.

At the end of 1931 Traeger, after the heavy work of that year, had travelled to Melbourne by train to knock at the door of the Chief of the Radio Branch. He had again put on his Sunday suit.

It was a strange skirmish to be undertaken by this quiet and reserved radio man, because John Flynn himself had always been the key negotiator with the communication bureaucrats. But this small man was no shirker when it came to facing up to the criticisms of officialdom. He seemed to possess an uncanny confidence that the pedal radio scheme was bound for ultimate success, and it was a new sight to see him in his Sunday clothes displaying his inner courage and determination to get proper recognition from the Government authorities.

On this particular occasion Traeger got to the desk of the Chief Inspector of Wireless Telegraphy. He returned to Adelaide with the optimistic report that he had won the day, and that the Post Master General's Department was giving permanent approval to the pedal radio scheme in spite of the fact that people in the outback homes were not licensed wireless operators.

However, this was not the end of serious dialogue with the Radio Branch, and during the next two years there were various exchanges of correspondence and

The Traeger Workshop.

some urgent personal overtures by Dr. George Simpson on Traeger's behalf – relating to licences, call signs, and transmission frequencies. Finally it came to be acknowledged by all parties that the goal and good sense of Traeger made his scheme uniquely professional for those times. Formal arrangements were confirmed about payment to the Australian Inland Mission for telegrams transmitted, approval was given for the regular registration of each pedal radio outpost by P.M.G. licence, and the unofficial privilege was granted to pedal radio operators to communicate with one another at certain times. The good grace of Mr. James Malone, the head of the Government Radio Branch, as well as his friendship with John Flynn, were important factors in getting the Traeger scheme properly on course from the official point of view.

Dr. George Simpson described the Traeger scheme as 'incapable of definition by rules and regulations'. And certainly on several occasions Traeger found himself installing a pedal set in the field before he had any official licence in his hand!

1933 was a critical year because it was the watershed period when experiments were being left behind and a permanently structured pattern of operation with improved equipment was evolving.

But the pressing problem of extensive field-work still had to be faced, while fresh requests were also coming not only from established outposts with orders for automatic keyboards but from all kinds of places where there were urgent needs.

Bob Gunther wrote from Monkira cattle station in the Diamantina River country north of Birdsville: "I am writing with regards to installing one of the wonderful transmitting sets that the A.I.M. are using with such success." He explained how his family were completely cut off for eight weeks by the wet the previous year. Cuthbert Hughes of Koolatah Station, halfway up to Cape York, wrote an imploring letter: "We are as good as dead up here," he said. Vic Hall, the policeman at Anthony Lagoon, sent a petition signed by 32 men at Timber Creek. He referred to several bush tragedies. There were letters from Blood's Creek, Coober Pedy, Daly River, a missionary in the new Hebrides, a boring contractor on the Murranji Track, Michael Patrick Durack on Ivanhoe station near Wynham, and Poddy Aiston of Mulka on the Birdsville Track. The Department of the Interior ordered four extra sets for the police in the Northern Territory. Harry Ding of Yunta, the Marree-Birdsville mail carrier, made enquiries about setting up his own miniature network.

On 29th April 1933 Traeger packed his bags and joined Kingsley and Gertrude Partridge in Alice Springs. The scheduled plan was to service and update the pedal sets already installed at Hermannsburg, Victoria River Downs, Borroloola, Anthony Lagoon, Mornington Island and Birdsville, and to make new installations at Elkedra, Groote Eylandt, Roper River, Koolatah and Delta. Three months on the road – wintertime May, June and July.

Traeger recalled this long stint of field-work with some candid comments. He had to sit in the back set of the Dodge car crowded with wireless gear. Kingsley Partridge now had his new bride with him. Traeger described himself as the 'awkward third party'. Their first call was to Hermannsburg. Traeger enjoyed this. The Partridges had not been to this Lutheran Mission where Traeger had previously established such warm friendships. Young Edwin Pareroultja again rushed up with welcoming wide eyes as Traeger was introducing 'Mr. And Mrs. Partridge' to Pastor Albrecht. A new frequency was fixed in the wireless set, and fresh brushes were set in place in the commutator of the pedal generator. Then they were on the road again. Traeger felt it was a very happy start. The next call was at Elkedra cattle station east of Alice Springs where the usual big job awaited them – the installation of a completely new pedal set and the erection of the high aerial pole and its four supporting guy posts. They got there next day after overnighting in Alice Springs. At smoko time Mrs. Partridge begged Traeger to call her 'Gertie'. He was quite taken aback in the presence of other people of the station, and typical of the man he said nothing but retained his regular formality for the whole three months they were together. He later laughingly made the comment: "When it came to camping on the roadside I always unrolled my swag a safe distance away. I wasn't used to travelling with honeymooners!"

Mrs. Partridge, not to be outdone, took a special interest in Traeger's radio work, and at the A.I.M. Hospital at Victoria River Downs she sat beside Sister

Francis sending Morse code and helped her to work the pedal generator. This outpost was the longest distance from Cloncurry in the whole network and there was excitement all round when Maurie Anderson answered their call.

Gertrude Partridge was overcome with wonderment, and this gladdened Traeger's heart. Here was a new, observant lady who quickly understood what it all meant. When they camped at the Katherine River a few days later she actually grabbed his two dirty shirts and washed them. But he still – and always – called her Mrs. Partridge!

The track up to the Cape York Peninsula country took the Partridge-Traeger party over the sandy crossings of the Staaten, Nassau and Mitchell Rivers, ending up at the isolated Koolatah cattle station. The Cuthbert Hughes family were cut off completely each year by the flooding monsoonal rains. The pedal wireless was duly installed and working. Cuthbert Hughes sent a typical letter with a cheque for £100 ($200) to the A.I.M. headquarters in Sydney. "Money can't buy," he wrote, "what the pedal radio has brought to our family. Also I can now find out the right times to send our bullocks to Chillagoe." Two months later an urgent call by pedal radio from Koolatah to the Flying Doctor saved the life of one of the family, even if the medical plane was not able to land on the station airstrip and the Flying Doctor had to wade across the Mitchell River.

While Traeger was installing the new pedal set at Delta Downs station, just north of the town of Normanton, for the veteran Sam Pointon and his family, the first item of news on the receiver was about the happenings at Groote Eylandt following the Caledon Bay massacres. In September 1932 three Aboriginal men at Caledon Bay on the north Arnhem Land coast had speared to death the entire crew of a Japanese lugger who were fishing on the coastline for trepang – that prized popular sea animal known as beche-de-mer.

It was Harold Shepherdson on his pedal wireless at Millingimbi who gave the news of the Caledon Bay murders to the world, otherwise the authorities in Darwin would have had to wait for weeks to get the story from the next Mission lugger.

The whole drama connected with the Caledon Bay happening had its beginnings in old-time history when boatloads of foreign fishermen, pearlers and traders invaded the waters and rivers of the Arnhem Land coast. Trading in women and alcohol eventually became a common practice and the Aboriginal elders could see that their very existence was at stake. The incident at Caledon Bay was probably inevitable.

A group of Aboriginal men had agreed to work for a Japanese crew of trepangers, but one upstanding black man openly refused. An angry brawl followed. Three Aboriginal fighters uncovered their spears hidden in the sand before the Japanese could get their guns. The total Japanese crew of six men were speared through their hearts.

Fred Gray, a 'white man fisherman', heard the story from an Aboriginal friend and he sailed the empty Japanese lugger to Millingimbi. Harold Shepherdson on his pedal radio Morse-coded the full story to the Commissioner of Police in Darwin. A series of dramatic events ensued. A police party was organised to capture the Aboriginal 'offenders of the law'. Constable Albert Stewart McColl was speared to death in the bush. Constable Jack Mahoney miraculously escaped being killed. The Aboriginal spear that seemed to come from nowhere cut his policeman's hat in half. The Methodist missionaries at Millingimbi and Goulburn Island tried to persuade the police party to forget their guns. The Anglican missionaries arranged an unarmed 'Peace Expedition' to try to promote an understanding between all parties. Traeger's pedal wireless at Groote Eylandt became the police medium of communication. One telegram had 200 words.

In the end 'the white-man fisherman' on the Caledon Bay coast, Fred Gray, came into the picture again. He met up with the unarmed 'Peace Expedition' of Anglican missionaries and offered to track down the three Aboriginal men who had killed the Japanese crew, and also Tuckian, who had speared Constable McColl.

An extraordinary event took place. On the sandy beach of Caledon Bay a kind of corroboree was held. The four offending Aboriginal men were persuaded to go to Darwin for the same kind of 'peace corroboree' with the Government. They preferred this action rather than having policemen in their country with guns.

The final trials and imprisonment in Darwin did not turn out to be a peace conference although it was first of all hailed as such in the Australian newspapers. Unfortunately, in the meantime there had been two further murders at Caledon Bay and calls for 'British justice' hit the headlines. Tuckian, the Aboriginal who had speared Constable McColl, was sentenced to death, and the three black men who had killed the Japanese crew were each given 20 years' imprisonment with hard labour. A later appeal, however, to the High Court gave Tuckian his freedom. The basic misunderstanding in the whole Caledon Bay happening seemed to be that the four Aboriginal men involved had joined the lugger to Darwin in the belief that they were to take part in a kind of 'corroboree peace talk' with the 'Government people'.

Traeger had received the first news of the Caledon massacre on the pedal wireless that he was installing at Delta Down cattle station, and three days later followed up the unfolding story at the Cloncurry mother station with Maurie Anderson. They got in contact with 'Sheppie' at Millingimbi. They quickly discovered what a central part had been played in the whole communication drama by the pedal wireless network. Traeger couldn't help but recall the incident at Mornington Island where the murder of the missionary Rev. Robert Hall had prompted John Flynn to give urgent priority to the Mornington Island people in guaranteeing them one of the first pedal wireless sets to be installed.

Following on his own experience at Hermannsburg and his deepening friendship with Pastor Albrecht, Traeger was developing what he called a 'real conscience' about helping Aboriginal communities. He knew that if there had been a pedal wireless in 1922 Pastor Carl Strehlow would not have died at Horsehoe Bend. Furthermore, he couldn't escape the nagging thought about the possibility of pedal wireless being used to conduct school lessons over the air for all bush children, including young Edwin Pareroultja and black youngsters like

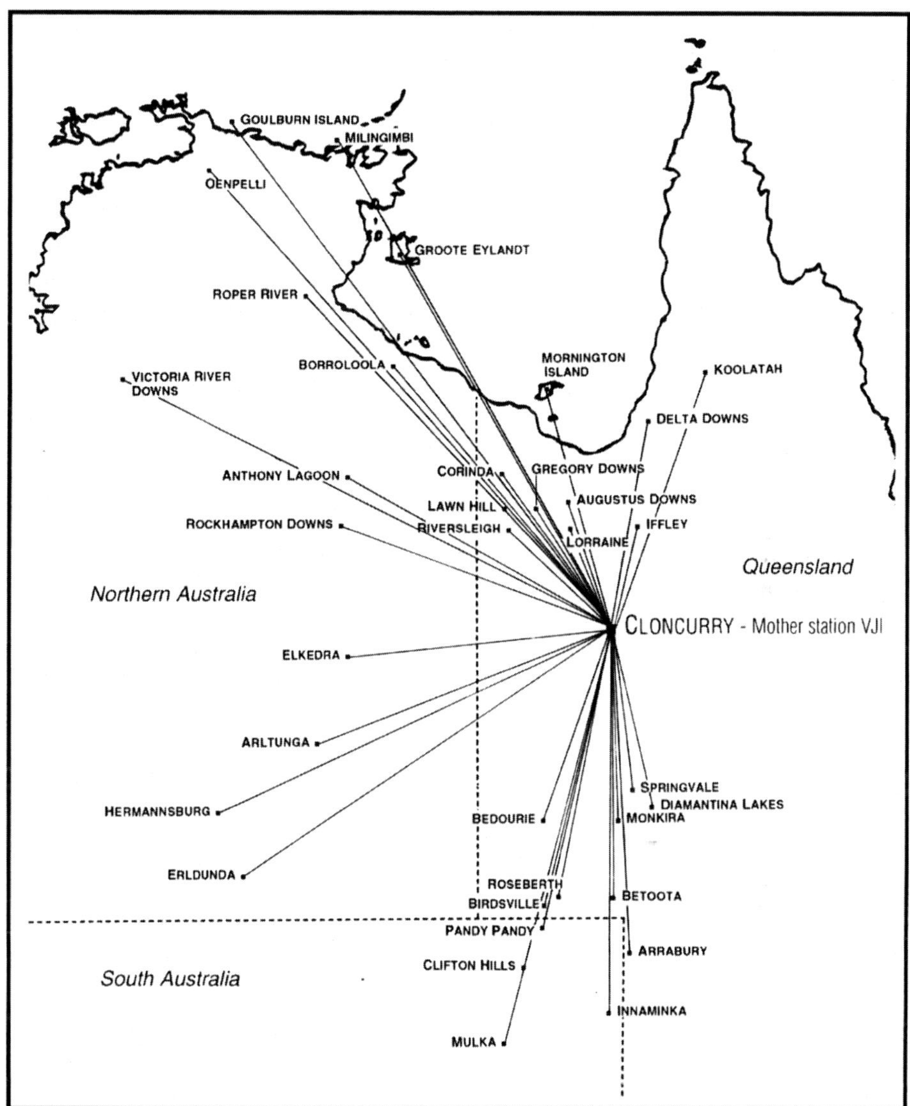

THE TRAEGER COMMUNICATION NETWORK 1929-1935

Within six years there were 40 pedal wireless outposts (including mobile sets) in daily contact with the base station in Cloncurry.

him. The first person, therefore, to rejoice when the School of the Air started in Alice Springs in 1951 was Traeger, then in his 56th year, who smiled and remembered his dreams 18 years before.

When Traeger got back to Adelaide he talked for long hours with his pastor at the Bethlehem Church. Pastor Janzow didn't know anything about Borroloola, Birdsville or Betoota, or about Groote Eylandt, Mornington Island or

Millingimbi, but he said he believed that God's hand was mysteriously upon every pedal wireless that went into these faraway places. Traeger said nothing but gave his typical chuckle.

Traeger was intrigued when the two latest nursing sisters at the Birdsville A.I.M. Hospital, Amy Bishop and Edna McLean, sent a note to him asking for a supply of new wire for their wireless aerials. They were being troubled by hordes of screeching galahs, those well-known pink-bodied and grey-winged cockatoos with big beaks and curled feet. Flocks of these persistent visitors were veering through the skies from the trees on the Diamantina River and landing with screeching precision on the swinging aerial wires stretching from the hospital roof to the top of the 20-metre-high piping pole in the yard. All this was too much for the sagging aerial wires, which were breaking and falling to the ground.

Traeger sent off two rolls of stronger wire and at the same time encouraged the sisters in their enquiry about starting an organised daily radio session with the women of the Diamantina River area. "Go ahead," he said, "the Post Master General says you can transmit on 148 metres if you fix your times with the base station in Cloncurry – and what about making your chatter to one another just like the galahs on your aerial?"

And so the famous 'Galah Session' came into being in 1935 as each pedal set in the Birdsville area was equipped to operate on voice. It was lucky that Bob Gaffney from the local hotel was able, on the technical side, to help to get it all going.

Each morning at 7 o'clock sharp Sister Amy Bishop called up the women at Clifton Hills, Pandy Pandy, The Bluff, Betoota, Bedourie and Monkira, and one by one they engaged in talking to one another about the happenings of the day and their family doings. Maurie Anderson in Cloncurry claimed it was the first talkback radio in Australia. Maybe in the world!

Galah Sessions became part of life in the far outback in Queensland, Western Australia, Central Australia, New South Wales and South Australia. This easy-going friendly talkback came to be looked upon as a life-saving daily contact, especially by the women on far-separated station properties.

Telephones were destined to take over from the high-frequency radio in later years, but it was natural that when this happened there would be sad hearts among hundreds of homemakers in the bush.

CHAPTER TWELVE

The New Flying Doctor Organisation

At the beginning of 1933 Rev. John Flynn began to talk with vigour and purpose about the future development of the Flying Doctor and Pedal Wireless Scheme. It was obvious to him that the emerging urgent challenge was to expand the so-called 'Mantle of Safety' Australia-wide. He was adamant in his thinking that this task was beyond the capacity and resources of a Church organisation like the Australian Inland Mission and that the whole national family of Australia should be part of a new independent movement.

There was a group within the Presbyterian Church who opposed this Flynnian hope and advocated in the General Assembly that their denomination should not surrender the success it had won in founding the Flying Doctor Service. Flynn made the quiet comment – "Since our Aerial Medical Service has won wide praise I can understand why there are people who would like to keep it within the Church" – but he went on to add his definite opinion that if it remained tied to its mother's apron strings the whole scheme could not possibly develop its potential strength.

Flynn's tact and wisdom won the support of the General Assembly in September 1933 when it approved that a new independent organisation of national character be created and that the Cloncurry A.I.M. Aerial Medical Service be transferred freely and completely to the new body.

Traeger had just returned to Adelaide from Marree after his long period of field-work. The A.I.M. office had posted him the General Assembly Minute. He sat down and read it with absorbing interest. He spoke to Rev. David Chapman, the South Australian member of the A.I.M. Board, who explained that Forgan Smith, the Premier of Queensland, after discussions with John Flynn had a month earlier presented a resolution to a Premiers' conference following which a plan was adopted by all States to work toward "an orderly development of a federal flying doctor organisation".

Traeger suddenly came to realise that radical changes were afoot. The prospect of losing his intimate bonds with the Australian Inland Mission set him thinking about his whole future career.

The news also came through about Flynn's action in Melbourne. It was probably the most momentous meeting Flynn had ever arranged. It took place in the banquet lounge of the old Victoria Palace in Little Collins Street. Flynn had rounded up 52 leading citizens of Melbourne. The Lord Major was persuaded to take the chair. It was three days before the Melbourne Cup of 1933. There were country people everywhere. This strategic conference, followed by an administrative meeting on 9th February 1934, set the compass for the new direction of the Flynn dream. The "Australian Aerial Medical Service" came into being. The Victorian section led the way, being officially registered on 23rd August 1934.

Traeger was inevitably being thrust into the lap of the new organisation. It was the natural course of events. For the time being, however, and until the end of 1937, he remained a paid staff member of the Australian Inland Mission, and it was natural that his main interests should continue to be centred on the progress being made among his special friends in the Cloncurry area who were using pedal sets. Cloncurry had been his pioneering domain. This was where his heart was. A succession of typical aerial masts pointing into the sky at homestead after homestead gave popular evidence that Traeger had passed that way. Indeed, he had the right to claim every one of them as part of himself.

Before departing altogether from the Cloncurry scene he had two pressing hopes. The first was to get every pedal set to operate on radio telephony as well as on the original Morse code. His ingenious automatic Morse keyboard had proved an extremely welcome boon for scores of bush people, but the Flying Doctor was becoming increasingly aware that in cases of extreme urgency it was difficult for many callers to communicate quickly and effectively in Morse code, and in addition there were some very humourous misreadings of messages.

On 10th September 1934 Traeger wrote triumphantly to the A.I.M. office saying he could immediately supply 'telephone equipment' for every pedal set in the Cloncurry network. It is pertinent to quote his letter because John Flynn was jubilant and wanted to know the details. "In simple technical terms," wrote Traeger, "the idea is a B class modulator fitted on to the standard transmitter with the improved type of transmitter valve fitted. The microphone currents are amplified and drive the modulator which in turn modulates the carrier wave supplied by the transmitter. All you have to do is to talk into the microphone while pedalling." John Flynn and David Wyles knew what Traeger was talking about even if other members of the A.I.M. Executive did not.

By 1935 Traeger's hope was realised. Radio telephony became a reality in the whole Cloncurry network. The 'Galah Session' at Birdsville pioneered talkback radio, and the Flying Doctor, mid-air in his new Fox Moth Aircraft, could keep in contact by voice with patients and callers on the ground anywhere. It was a consummating triumph for Traeger. Everybody could now really talk with one another.

His second hope related to the mother station in Cloncurry. During November-December 1934 he had been able to work with Maurie Anderson and Vernon Kerr and almost completely rebuild the station, with increased power and new equipment enabling it to transmit to an increased number of pedal sets in the field. By the end of 1935, VJI Cloncurry and approximately 50 pedal wireless outposts had consolidated their permanent pattern of efficient operation[9]. Traeger's second urgent hope was fulfilled.

The first commission given to Traeger by the new organisation was to build the base radio stations at Port Hedland in the Pilbara region for the Western Australian section and at Wyndham in the Kimberley area for the Victorian section. He contracted to do this for £1000 ($2000) for each base in September-October 1935.

When he had completed the building of the two sets of radio equipment in his Adelaide workshop he shipped the loads, including the aerial masts, to Port Hedland and Wyndham. The responsibility connected with these installations in totally unknown territory and among new people was one of the most unpredictable tasks yet undertaken by Traeger. He was now 40 years of age. He travelled by train to Perth and caught the boat at Fremantle on this land and sea venture.

The pastoral firm of Dalgety's had paid for the total transport of the two loads of wireless gear and had advised Traeger of its safe arrival at each of the destinations.

As Traeger climbed off the ship in Port Hedland in mid-September his first thoughts were not about radio installations but about a lady. By a strange irony in the character of the radio man he had developed a deeply felt companionship with the warmhearted nursing sister Gwen Pearson whom he had met at the Birdsville A.I.M. Hospital. Traeger was well aware that when she had completed her term at Birdsville she went the extra mile by volunteering to go to the A.I.M. Hospital at Port Hedland with a fellow Queenslander, Sister Thelma Reid.

Sister Gwen Pearson had gone though the traumatic experience in Birdsville with the tragic death of her companion Sister Maude Gilbert and of Jesse Shackleton, Traeger's offsider. She had wept in Traeger's arms. In the dark of the lonely Birdsville street before Traeger set off on his solitary trip back to Cloncurry they had shared their hurt and grief together. On his arrival in Port Hedland nearly six years later he booked in at the Pier Hotel and went straight to the hospital. On the verandah of the nurses quarters they sat together. He took her in

9 The operating frequencies were popularly described as Short, Medium and Long Waves – 34.7 metres (8630 Kcs) 58.7 metres (3110 Kcs) 148 metres (2020.5 Kcs).

During the period 1936-1940, 37 Traeger pedal sets with both Morse code and telephony capacities were in operation in the Port Hedland and Wyndham networks carrying the new 'Australian Aerial Medical Services' name plate.

This same model carrying the 'Transceiver' name plate was the updated and popular pedal set in the Cloncurry network during the same period. Transmitting power was still supplied by pedal generators. Valves were supplied by Philips Lamps Australia as acknowledged on all official name plates since the year 1936.

his arms again. Gwen Pearson was one A.I.M. nurse who caught a light in Alfred Traeger's eyes.

After the completion of the Port Hedland radio base, Fred Hull became the radio operator whose name became a household word throughout the Pilbara region. Traeger installed the first pedal radio in Western Australia at Warrawagine station, 225 kilometres inland, and on the very first day an urgent call was made to the Flying Doctor to save the life of an Aboriginal who had broken his back. Within a year there were 25 Traeger pedal sets successfully operating in the Port Hedland network.

From Port Hedland Traeger proceeded to Wyndham, the most northern cattle port on the Kimberley coastline. By the end of September the base station was ready. G.I. Guppy took over as the first operator. By the time an official opening took place Traeger had 12 pedal sets operating in the region – Noonkanbah, Mt. House, Koolan Island, Cape Leveque, Daly River, Timber Creek, Argyle, Inverway, Waterloo, Fort George, Balfour Downs and Forrest River Mission.

This marked the beginning of Traeger's involvement with the wireless world of the new national organisation.

Although Traeger had little association with the practical processes and legal constitutions of the various new sections of the Australian Aerial Medical Service he played a real part in the 'big transfer' of the Cloncurry wireless network to the new organisation. He quite forcibly claimed that a radio person should be present at the inaugural meeting of the Brisbane people who were to comprise the Council of the Queensland section of the A.A.M.S. Maurie Anderson was already preparing to go to Alice Springs to found the wireless base there, and Vernon Kerr accordingly became the wireless representative and sat beside John Flynn at the unforgettable meeting in Brisbane on 26th April 1939.

It turned out that Kerr was the only person present who could provide up-to-date information on the series of pedal sets and other equipment that were the acknowledged property of the Australian Inland Mission. Rev. John Flynn, who had actually planned the selection of every member of the new Council, headed by the stalwart cattleman Norman Bourke, forestalled everybody because he was able to convey the decision of the Board of the Australian Inland Mission to hand over completely and freely the total radio property and equipment connected with the Cloncurry network. Vernon Kerr was able to confirm that the three people on the radio staff, Maurie Anderson, Miss Ethel Hooker and himself, would spontaneously become employees of the Queensland section. On the medical side a similar decision was made. From the operational point of view therefore, the so-called 'Big Transfer' became a very simple process and a new Secretariat was set up in Brisbane to take over administrative controls.

When World War II broke out five months later the Flying Doctor service was a truly national organisation. The news of the declaration of war by Prime Minister Robert Menzies was spread up and down the tracks of the outback on Traeger's pedal wireless.

CHAPTER THIRTEEN

The Unexpected Happening

Before the handover of the Cloncurry base station to the newly created Flying Doctor organisation, John Flynn undertook a final round-up trip in the Gulf area with Fred McKay. In mid-July 1937 they spent a day with the Black family at Eddington Station near Julia Creek. Flynn wrote a letter to Alf Traeger, which he posted in Normanton on the way to the cattle properties in the Cape York Peninsula country. The letter was a typical Flynn epistle, probably the last one he wrote to his radio man, and it was written for an exceptionally personal reason.

In April 1934 there had been a vital disagreement between these two very close friends. Flynn had made a radical proposal that could have changed Traeger's entire career. On 10th April the Assistant Manager of the firm of Amalgamated Wireless of Australia (A.W.A.) had informed Flynn and his A.I.M. Board that they had now manufactured a pedal wireless similar to the Traeger machine and were selling it in New Guinea. Flynn, in consultation with A.W.A., thereupon had evolved a plan that he believed would be an advantage in the future development of the Flying Doctor radio work, namely that A.W.A. would take over the complete production of pedal sets with Traeger employed as a member of staff.

Flynn sent a telegram to Traeger: "Come to Sydney immediately. All expenses paid. Have arranged plan of great advantage to yourself and A.I.M." Traeger caught the train to Melbourne where his 'wireless godfather' Harry Kauper was now working. Kauper had already gleaned some of the details of the plan that

Flynn had in mind and he quickly shared his strong belief with Traeger that the scheme would rob the Cloncurry network of its important family spirit and its well-established simple mode of operation.

There had also been some background problems with A.W.A. relating to the patent rights of radio equipment, and Traeger had become acutely aware of the implications of these problems in view of the prospect of future sales of his pedal sets.

When he arrived in Sydney he immediately made contact with his friends in Philips Lamps Ltd who were already supplying him with radio valves and other equipment at reduced cost. Armed with a signed document that all future Traeger Transceivers would be built and marketed 'under licence from Philips Lamps' he went to the meeting that Flynn had arranged with A.W.A. When Flynn saw that Traeger was not interested in 'throwing in his lot with A.W.A.' and had already gained a contract with Philips he became visibly agitated and upset. Traeger later wrote an account of this confrontation because it was an unusual and critical episode in his life. He described Flynn as being 'very angry', and their relationship for the time being certainly lost its old-time cordiality.

Flynn three years later was at Eddington station writing a letter to Traeger. It was a note of renewal of fatherly sentiment and gratitude with an expression of good wishes in the new era of service that Traeger was facing. This letter did more than simply revive the memories of their pioneering radio experiments together in Cloncurry in 1927. Traeger was quietly nurturing in his mind another surprising enterprise, and Flynn's letter helped him to believe that the benediction of his old boss would be wholeheartedly given.

It was the most unpredictable happening in Traeger's life. He was thinking about getting married.

His devout mother, prompted by her strong home-making ideals, was praying that her 42-year-old son would soon follow the normal family tradition and find a good Lutheran wife.

There were also other influences at this time that crossed Traeger's path and that played a decisive part in his thinking about the future. These influences came from his own mates, his wireless co-workers, particularly in Cloncurry. He worked beside Maurie Anderson, who was at the same time courting a vivacious girl, Meg Burness, and he rejoiced at their marriage. He saw the love drama unfold when Joy Elton came to Cloncurry and won the heart of Vernon Kerr even in the midst of his heavy radio work, the subsequent wedding party being one of the most popular in town. Traeger, in spite of his reserved and shy character, was coming to see that his daily workmates were joyfully entering into inspiring feminine partnerships – and this was happening in an intimate way before his very eyes.

In addition he saw the happy union of Dr. Allan Vickers and Lilias Whitman, the chemist's daughter. Vickers shared his exciting story while Traeger and Anderson were installing the radio equipment in the Flying Doctor plane. Even Jean Baird, who handled all the radio licences at headquarters for Traeger, had married John Flynn – 'the boss'. And Traeger, on his visit to Port Hedland, had seen the happiness that Bob Ellery was bringing into the life of Gwen Pearson, the Birdsville Sister who had wept in his arms.

Traeger back in Adelaide bought a block of land at 64 Godfrey Terrace, Erindale. He then followed up by engaging a well-known carpenter from the Bethlehem Church congregation to build a home.

During the same month Traeger received a special commission from the A.I.M. to build two portable transceivers with the latest improvements. This was extremely gratifying to Traeger because these final tasks for the A.I.M. stirred up vivid recollections of the early days. He was also keen to show that his pedal generator could still do an efficient job while the experts were talking about the big changes that would soon come with vibrator models.

These two special mobile sets were for the use of patrol padres in Queensland. The first one was railed to Cloncurry for the far western Queensland patrol in February 1937. This portable pedal set travelled in a truck for thousands of miles for four years covering the entire area of the Cloncurry wireless network. Its performance in the field was exceptional, breaking records for daily traffic and medical calls. It was used by Flynn while travelling on his last field round-up for a whole series of important telegrams relating to the creation of the national Flying Doctor body.

The life-saving effectiveness of this particular Traeger portable pedal set is well illustrated in a story told by Margaret McKay:

"We were travelling in the patrol truck God knows where! It was a lonely unmarked track out hear Haddon Corner where the Queensland border fence takes its right-angle turn towards Innamincka country. We were trying to get to Betoota and then to Birdsville. The regular road was flooded. As our truck bumped its way into a rocky creek bed the off-side front wheel collapsed with the driving gear broken and the king pin smashed in two. Some repair work was carried out but with no replacement king pin we were hopelessly stranded – except for our Traeger pedal wireless. There was a solitary whitewood tree some distance away. Fred carried the pedal set by its leather straps and threw the random aerial wire over the top of the whitewood tree. He sat on a biscuit tin and pedalled with the transmitter tuned to the shortwave frequency. The Cloncurry Flying Doctor Base picked up the distress call – about 800 miles away. Maurie Anderson the operator quickly took down particulars. The nearest point of contact was with Tanbar cattle station, about ninety miles from our breakdown site. Maurie Anderson helped to work the miracle. He had to get information to the Post Office at Windorah, about 200 miles from where we were – by telegraph to Townsville, Brisbane, Charleville and finally to Windorah where the Post Master on an erratic bush telephone line got through to Mr. Doug McFarlane the Manager of Tanbar station. We were stranded for three days. On the fourth day Fred got me settled with the pedal radio and some tinned sardines and not knowing that a message had actually got through to Tanbar started to walk for help carrying a water bag and food. After covering about ten miles he met Doug McFarlane of Tanbar coming to the rescue with spare parts and a hamper of meat sandwiches. The final details of the story don't matter. The plain fact was that next

"Our parents wouldn't let us go on such a big journey unless we had a pedal wireless" – (Frances Rycen). Eight children (from left: Frances Rycen, Bill Lauder, Hazel Lauder, Doris Tunney, Dick Norton, Joyce Rycen, Gladys Norton) would never have got the chance of a seaside holiday unless Traeger provided the pedal wireless to give them daily security on a daring 2000-kilometre trip in an open truck.

day we were back at Tanbar station with a repaired truck safe and sound. For me it was a never-to-be-forgotten happening. Traeger's portable pedal wireless was a life-saver! I couldn't keep back the tears as I thanked God for Traeger and his midget miracle machine."

A remarkable story is also told by eight children who were conveyed by open truck from Trekelano in far western Queensland to Brisbane in connection with the Bush Children's Health Scheme. This long journey by road was made practicable only because each day the parents were assured by pedal radio that their children were safe. One boy in the group was only six years of age and his mother each morning wanted to know if he was still crying! When Traeger heard the story he quietly commented that one of the real purposes of the pedal wireless was to 'help the kids of the bush'.

It was the same sort of human feeling that gripped Traeger as in his workshop he recalled the lively picture of his 'wireless mates' in Cloncurry finding lady helpmates to be part of their lives. It appears that he himself had never seriously contemplated the joys of marriage and a fireside of his own. The time had come, however, when his stature as the inventor of the pedal wireless was being publicly recognised, and when people, even ladies in the local Bethlehem Church, were expressing pride to be in his company.

Olga Schodde, a regular lady of the congregation, made sure that she sat in the pew behind Traeger in church and she developed the thoughtful habit of inviting Alf and his brother Jack to her home for lunch each Sunday. The friendship grew.

The home in Godfrey Terrace was completed. Alf bought a new suit. The wedding took place in the Bethlehem Church on 11th September 1937. Pastor William Janzow gave the couple a special benediction. It was a good, robust Lutheran celebration. The radio mates in Cloncurry were overjoyed and sent congratulations in Morse code. Messages of good wishes came from 22 pedal wireless outposts. Rev. John Flynn sent a typical telegram – 'Mobs of Blessings'.

Traeger was now a married man rushing around and buying furniture for his new home.

In the Traeger workshop there were also big changes. The long-standing official ties with the Australian Inland Mission ended two months after the wedding, and Traeger from that date became an independent radio contractor specialising in work for the new Flying Doctor organisation.

He set up a new factory in a simple rectangular building at 11 Dudley Street, Marryatville. Jack Drew, an experienced radio engineer and a special friend, offered to join Traeger's team as Assistant Manager. The title "Traeger Transceivers" was painted in capital letters on a white signboard at the front entrance.

CHAPTER FOURTEEN

War And Post-War

The 12 years of unrelenting pace – 'as busy as an ant' as Traeger put it – were over. A refreshing sense of independent freedom gripped him as he realised that his basic radio communication scheme was now established and a going concern. Flynn's dream was walking, talking and flying.

Shortly after the war broke out there were over 200 pedal wireless outposts in regular operation, and fresh orders were coming in from the new bases at Broken Hill, Alice Springs and Western Australia. The Traeger Transceiver workshop at Marryatville was alive with activity. For Alf himself it was a new role to be the managing director of a commercial operation. The old time image of a farming lad in trousers held up by striped braces was gone!

After setting up the Marryatville factory with new lighting and an improved range of technical equipment, his first task was to upgrade all the transceiver sets in the field so that they could operate with so-called 'vibrator supplies'. His nine mechanical helpers with Jack Drew at the head made a keen working team. The idea of the so-called 'vibrator unit' was to replace the pedal generator with a mechanical device to obtain high-tension, direct-current electrical power from a six-volt car battery. This radio procedure was not a new one, but Traeger could not harness vibrator supplies for his transceiver until there was guaranteed common access to these batteries in the outback.

The vibrator unit did not merely replace the pedal generator in supplying high-tension current to the transmitter. It also delivered high-tension power for the receiver valves, eliminating B batteries altogether. Once Traeger announced that he had vibrator sets on the production line there were urgent requests again

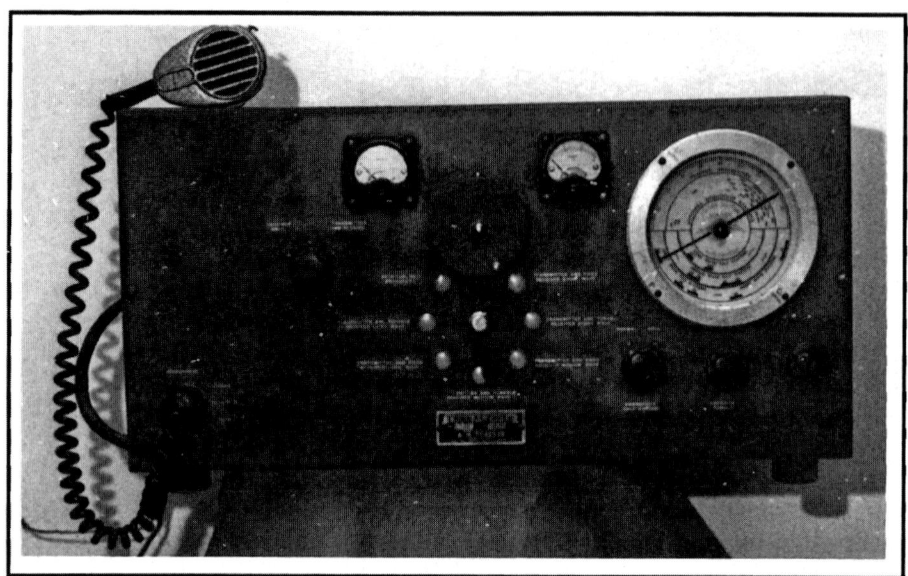

The popular war and post-war Traeger vibrator set with power provided by a six-volt high-tension battery. By the mid-war years (c. 1943) the historic pedal generators were replaced by vibrator supplies and Morse code was no longer a necessary provision.

from the outpost people. Although the bush operators continued to speak about sending messages 'on the pedal' the installation of hundreds of vibrator sets quickly created a new age in bush communication[10].

It came as a surprise to the people who operated Traeger wireless sets in the northern sectors of the Cloncurry and Wyndham networks that they should become 'front line troops' when the Japanese fighters and bombers started to make their air attacks on Darwin and Broome.

From Warrawagine station near Port Hedland to Millingimbi in Arnhem Land there was a scattered chain of Traeger pedal wireless outposts. They almost automatically became important military 'watchdogs' in the North Australian Army Observation Corps under the command of an expert radio officer, Major Basil Hall.

Traeger was now in his mid-40s. He retained in his mind some sore memories of World War I when the Army Recruiting Agency excluded him from military service because of his German ancestry. However, he was now sought out by the army heads who urgently required communication services along the North Australian coastline.

Maurie Anderson, who had moved from Cloncurry in 1939 to open the radio base in Alice Springs, was recruited to join Major Hall's secret contingent.

10 In the Appendix a general description is given of the vibrator transceiver that Traeger introduced to replace the original pedal set.

Anderson and Traeger were the key people who were able to supply up-to-the minute information about the Flying Doctor radio networks, and also carry out urgent conversions of certain pedal sets into vibrator models.

The detailed story of the secret intelligence work carried out by the 'Basil Hall Boys' in all kinds of hazardous places has never been told, nor the part played by Traeger wireless sets.

Back in his workshop in later times Traeger continued to maintain a personal grief for his long-standing radio mate Maurie Anderson, who died from the severe disabilities he suffered from his so-called 'watchdog wireless service' in the crocodile country of the tropical north.

In the midst of workshop and wartime demands there were other special happenings in the Traeger home. Two children, Pauline Elizabeth and Anne Catherine, had come to romp on their floor. There were good Lutheran parties in the Bethlehem Church when the children were baptised. To Alf and his wife Olga they were high and sacred occasions. The fact that he was suddenly widowed when Pauline was eight years of age and Anne was six, meant that Alf then had the full caring responsibilities of a single parent. This, he admitted, was a very grim and exacting period in his life. Pauline and Anne never forgot his guiding hand and practical devotion.

Dr. George Simpson came to see Traeger at his workbench at Marryatville and to share the exploits of Dr. Neil Duncan who, after being the Flying Doctor in Cloncurry, had gone to pioneer an aerial medical service in Africa on the John Flynn pattern. Radio communication was urgently necessary, Simpson explained. Within a month Dr. George Simpson was able to get details of the technical requirements from Dr Neil Duncan in Nigeria. Traeger inspired Jack Drew and his workshop team to face an almost impossible task.

Traeger urgently made blueprints of a completely new framework for the pedal set suitable for operation in Africa. Within six months 20 of these expertly constructed machines were shipped in a special container from Port Adelaide to Lagos, the capital of Nigeria.

Traeger was no seeker of silver or gold. The bill he sent to the new Flying Doctor organisation in Nigeria

In the midst of his Australian programme of building the new vibrator sets Traeger responded to an urgent request to build a special type of pedal set (TK2) for use in Africa. Twenty of these sets were shipped to Lagos for a Flying Doctor scheme in Nigeria.

Flying Doctor at his daily work on the new Traeger vibrator wireless set. The Doctor has completed a clinic session at White Cliffs (Broken Hill) and then carries out a consultation with another station about a patient needing medical help. This picture illustrates the fully developed process of telephony contact on an updated Traeger vibrator set with the R.F.D.S. medical chest on hand for nearby reference.

(Photo: Australian News and Information Bureau.)

did not recoup costs. Such actions were typical of the man because Traeger was never bound by strict accountancy practices. Nor could he ever erase from his mind the memories of the dismal conditions of the Great Depression days when he was installing many of the first pedal sets for the Australian Inland Mission as straight-out gifts to needy people. Indeed it was difficult for him to comprehend the quickly changed economic climate of the bustling post-war period, and particularly the upsurge of money-making activities in the field of mechanical engineering. All kinds of spare parts for cars, trucks and tractors were being produced in newly set-up small business ventures by returned service men who had learned fresh skills in wartime. The ingenious rotary lawn mower had a booming market. The great Snowy Mountains Scheme was forging ahead. The new Australian car, the Holden, was coming off the production line in hundreds.

Two-tone emergency whistle to call Flying Doctor at night.

Traeger had no public relations agency. Not even a full-time bookkeeper to keep his accounts in order. No one to advise him on the expanding field of competitors in the radio world. His simple goal was to have at least 500 Traeger Transceivers in active operation in bush homes from end to end of the isolated areas of Australia by the late 1960s.

This goal was a Traeger triumph. In the most distant Flying Doctor section of Eastern Goldfields (Kalgoorlie), for instance, in 1962 there were approximately 70 fixed outposts and several hundred portables, all of them being used by the Country Women's Association, the School of the Air, and the Isolated Children's Parents Association, as well as by the Flying Doctors. Traeger had a map on the wall in his workshop to prove that the gaps in Flynn's original dream were now being finally bridged. He pointed to the School of the Air record at Charleville Base. "Three hundred children on the daily roll call." Traeger had a rightful pride as he got his two children, now high school girls, to listen in to the Alice Springs School of the Air. This historic experiment of school teaching by air is today completely upgraded by the Distant Education Scheme, which is giving young people the best chance they have ever had of primary and secondary schooling by air. This unique movement started with Traeger pedal sets.

There was another revealing noticeboard in his Marryatville workshop. On this board were carefully recorded the names of all the radio operators at the various Flying Doctor base stations. Traeger frequently referred to the extraordinary bonds of friendship that existed between the 'radio boys' as he called them. Radio 'hams', no matter where they lived, were a 'connection' that set them apart as a unique fraternity. There were a select few of these pedal radio mates to whom Alf owed an immeasurable debt. They had shared his battle under difficult weather conditions with unending patience and often with inadequate equipment. His kinship with them was deep and personal. Traeger never forgot that the success of his pedal radio scheme largely depended on their dedication and efficiency.

One of the very early radio questions which Traeger had inevitably to face was – "What happens with an urgent medical case at night-time when the mother station is closed down?". He solved the problem with a tin whistle! First it was a handmade single tone whistle that rang an alarm at the base when blown for a few seconds into the microphone with the transmitter in action. Traeger went on to refine this ingenious device, making it more efficient with two tones. The mode of operation was to keep the fingers clear of the two holes in the whistle and blow for four seconds, and them immediately place a finger firmly at the end of the whistle and blow another six seconds. The decoder at the base station

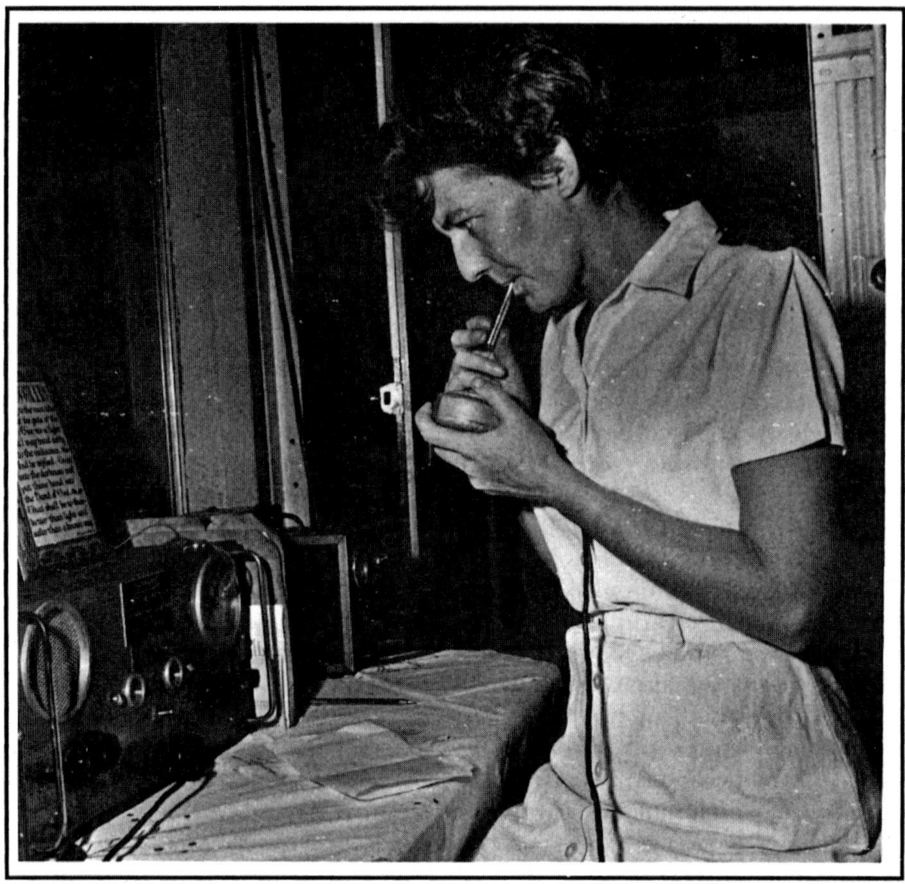

Sister Rosemary Ware, Fitzroy Crossing A.I.M. Hospital, calling up the Flying Doctor in Derby on the two-tone emergency whistle.

immediately released an electrical impulse that tripped a relay and rang an alarm bell. The base operator would wake up, turn on his transmitter and respond to the call. This typical innovative device meant that medical emergencies could be dealt with at any time of night. Nursing Sister Rosemary Ware wrote a report detailing the night-time occasions when Traeger's tin whistle saved the lives of 10 dangerously ill patients during her two-year term of nursing at Fitzroy Crossing Hospital.

When single side band radio equipment later became the order of the day a new system of alarm was incorporated in the whole radio circuit, but Traeger's tin-whistle mechanism in the meantime had been a simple miracle worker for a period of nearly 16 years. In the midst of his tin-whistle experiments Traeger got the surprise of his life to be invited to Government House Adelaide to be invested as an Officer of the Order of the British Empire. Traeger was flustered, but he went and bought his second new suit!

CHAPTER FIFTEEN

From 'Body Charts' To 'Single Side-Band'

Traeger though it was a joke! Fred Hull, the radio operator of the Flying Doctor base at Port Hedland, had posted him a letter enclosing a drawing of a human body with a sequence of numbers on it.

There was a twinkle on Alf's face as he read Hull's letter explaining that this so-called 'Body Chart' was now being used by the Flying Doctors at Port Hedland and Wyndham in their radio consultations with people who called for medical help.

It was the bright ideas of an enterprising nursing sister, Lucy Garlick (now Mrs. Johnstone). She made the initial neat drawing of the human body and pencilled numbers on the various physical areas so that when an outpost person needed the Flying Doctor he would be able to immediately to ask: "Where is the pain?".

This straightforward procedure became a natural part of the Traeger wireless network in every section of the Flying Doctor Service throughout Australia. The sheer simplicity of the body chart fascinated Traeger. He saw good humour and workaday effectiveness in it for both black and white people. It was as absurdly simple as the pedal wireless itself. And when artists got to work on designing the new $20 note in 1994 they couldn't avoid highlighting the body chart as an ingenious symbol of pedal radio communication by Flying Doctors. A nursing sister's pioneering drawing has therefore become a kind of historic icon of the sky doctor at work.

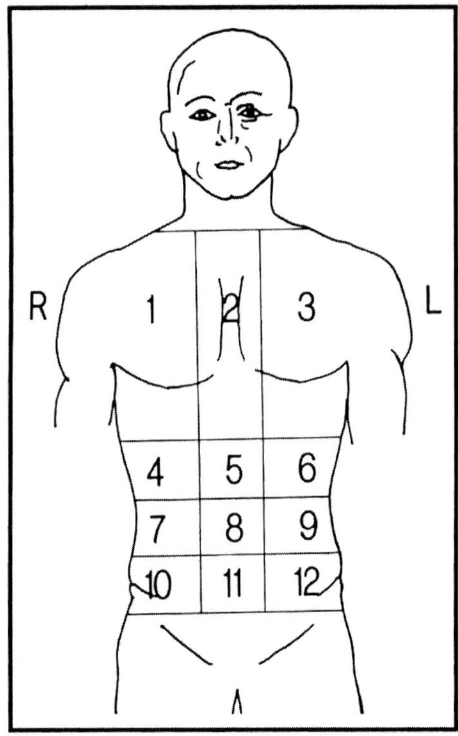

"Traeger thought it was a joke!"
The body chart became an ingenious symbol of pedal radio communication by flying doctors. "Where is the pain?"

It was a natural happening that the body chart should be coupled with the standard medical chest that the Flying Doctor leaders supplied to every outback wireless outpost. This was a lockable steel box with a series of shelves that initially contained 95 neatly numbered medicines and drugs. The contents of the chest were regularly reviewed by the Flying Doctor, and in addition to medicines there were bandages, dressings, hypodermic syringes, a scalpel, scissors, a kidney dish and a catheter. About 40 items were drugs marked 'Doctor's Orders Only'.

Flying Doctor Keith Sweetman of the Wyndham Base and Dr. George Simpson of the Victorian Flying Doctor Council were the instigators of the scheme, and by the 1960s there were 2000 medical chests and body charts in the widely scattered outback homes in the Traeger radio network.

Dr. George Simpson had also arranged for a medical chest and body chart to be placed in Traeger's workshop in Marryatville. This was Alf's personal wish because it enabled him and his team of workers to know what was going on in the bush areas, and even to tune into the radio base at Port Augusta and listen to their special friend Graham Pitts and the Flying Doctor making reference to medical chests and body charts in their daily medical calls. The people 'out there' were always Traeger's absorbing concern, and he would laugh quizzically at the story of the Flying Doctor who prescribed to a reputable old bushman that he should take two pills from bottle number 9 in the medical chest. The bushman reported back at the next radio session explaining that the number 9 bottle was empty but he had taken pills from number 7 and number 2 and was 'now feeling pretty good'.

These amusing stories about comical exchanges 'on the pedal' have become part of the folklore of the outback – rugged talkback yarns by drovers, the romance of the stockman trying to make love in Morse code, and vivid tales about women buying new things for the races. Even the crazy story about the distressed lady describing to the Flying Doctor on the radio the physical symptoms of her sick duck, which was "having terrible trouble laying its first egg!". These human happenings gave Traeger a kind of twinkling pleasure because they were down-to-earth proof of the fulfillment of Flynn's dream. Isolated people now had an everyday contact with the Flying Doctor and with one another. For that day and age in Australian outback history this was a technical wonder!

The remarkable fact is that Traeger's life goal never changed. Yet he was no visionary of the past and maintained an uncommon initiative in keeping abreast of the up-to-date developments in the radio world. He was an ardent reader of journals and books. However, at heart his sentiments had become intertwined with the lives of people in the bush. He consistently remained a sharer of their battles, and indeed of their sufferings. This was part of his earthy religious belief. His own words were: "I have always believed that God guided my life." Financial gain or merchandising on the open market were never part of his thinking or hopes.

In April 1956 Traeger, 60 years of age, faced a heart-rending dilemma. He wanted to accept. Emotionally he could not face it. It was the official invitation to the historic opening of the Memorial Church in Alice Springs on 5th May, the fifth anniversary of the death of John Flynn. The Governor General of Australia with a message from the Queen would be there. The Moderator General of the Presbyterian Church, the heads of other denominations and the Royal Flying Doctor Service, Mrs. Flynn and a multitude of dignitaries would be assembled on the main platform. Traeger was to have an honoured seat with the official party. After three sleepless nights he worried himself into a state of emotional turmoil. The very thought of the occasion, the officials, the crowds of people participating in the ceremony – made him feel physically unwell. This was typical of the extreme reserve of the man. He telephoned the Head Office of the Australian Inland Mission and bluntly said: "Dr. Duguid says I will be sick if I go. I will make a trip later sometime."

Traeger's historic original pedal set was a prime exhibit in the John Flynn Memorial Church museum on the day of the official opening. In his workshop in the distance Alf listened to the ceremony on the A.B.C. broadcast and in his mind's eye pictured the exciting day in 1926 when he and John Flynn carried out their first radio experiments on the very site where the Memorial Church was now standing. He gave a smiling nod of approval as he listened to the words of dedication spoken by the Moderator General.

In the '50s and '60s the post-war technical advances were catching up with people everywhere. In the radio world solid-state circuits as well as greatly improved batteries were bringing in a new era. Even everyday mechanical equipment was being changed radically by new plastics and light-metal alloys, and Traeger's mates in the inland were all driving new four-wheel drive vehicles. In the face of these developments and of his increasing age it was natural that Traeger should more and more delegate to Jack Drew the daily management of the Transceiver workshop. This meant that Alf himself was able to adopt a more unhurried pace of life and work. He had always been interested in archaeology. Now was his chance to get books from the library. Pastor Harold Koehne of the Bethlehem Church was conducting a monthly Bible study group for the Men's Association. Alf jumped at the chance of attending this study group to discover all he could about biblical archaeology. He bought a new tape recorder and never missed a word of Pastor Koehne's talks.

Saturday became a ritual tennis day. Daughters Pauline and Anne had developed into keen players following in their mother's footsteps. On a sunny Saturday in January 1956 Alf drove the two girls to a tennis match at Colonel Light Gardens. A bright-eyed lady, Joyce Edna Mibus, who had been widowed two years previously, was playing in the Bethlehem Church team. She and Alf talked together at the end of the match. It was a moment of destiny. Their eventual marriage was made in heaven. Joyce typed Alf's tapes from the Bible study group. Their common interests were deep seated and of the spirit. The wedding took place on Traeger's 61st birthday, 2nd August 1956, in the Colonel Light Gardens Lutheran Church.

The next 20 years brought a renewed sense of companionship into Traeger's life. On 13th March 1958 a son, Michael John, was born. Alf displayed an ecstasy that his Lutheran mates shared with laughter and joy. A refreshed sense of spiritual buoyancy came into his life as he now gave full priority to the nurturing of his son. On the week Michael was born he was enrolled for his complete education at Concordia, the big Lutheran School where in due course, like his father, he showed special gifts in mathematics and science, and where at the age of 14 years he was confirmed in the Christian faith according to the strict faith of the Lutheran Church. Alf himself was not slow at displaying openly that he had no misgivings about the inner priorities within his own life. He vigorously encouraged Michael in his religious commitments, recalling his own personal experience at the age of 14 years when his parents had sent him from their home at Balaclava to live for a month with friends in Adelaide and to attend weekly classes leading up to the service of confirmation.

When Michael was well established at Concordia College Alf, now strongly supported by Joyce in everything he did, made the big decision to retrace some of his old steps in the outback. In July 1969 they joined a coach party on

A renewed sense of companionship.

a 10-day visit to Alice Springs. They knew what to look for – the spacious area named 'Traeger Park' and the handsome bronze direction-finder 'commemorating Alfred Traeger' at the airport. Joyce proudly took photographs. They sat in the John Flynn Church. It was built on the very site where Traeger had erected his first wireless aerial pole in 1926. In the engine room at the rear of Adelaide House (the old A.I.M. Hospital building) Alf painted the memory scene of the pioneer mother station. At Hermannsburg Pastor Albrecht had gone, but Edwin Pareroultja, nearly 60 years of age and grey-haired was there. Joyce had tears in her eyes as the two men greeted one another. 'Alice Springs Revisited' was memorable. It was the place where Alf had caught the Flynn dream that set the course for his whole life.

A month later Alf and Joyce resolved to go by air to Cloncurry. They stood in front of the site in Uhr Street where St. Cuthbert's Presbyterian Church had once stood. This was Traeger's old 'hunting ground'. In the allotment a Memorial Cloister had now been erected with plaques affixed to a series of cement brick walls commemorating the historical events of the founding days of the aerial medical and wireless work. The dedication service for the Memorial Cloister took place on Saturday 17th August. Alf and Joyce stood with quiet pride among the 300 people as they sang without pomp or music 'O God our help in ages past'. Some of the old Cloncurryites shook Alf's hand with typical vigour as they recalled the Melbourne Cup day of 1927!

In October 1969 the reports of the Radio Committee of the Federal Council of the Flying Doctor Service came into Traeger's hands. This special Committee comprising the wireless experts George Pither (Victoria), Len Schultz (N.S.W.), Clive Pearce (Queensland) and later joined by Mr. Vern Kenna (N.S.W.), W.R. Grunow (Victoria) and Fred Hull (West Australia), were to lead the whole Flying Doctor organisation into the most revolutionary change it has yet faced in its radio history.

In 1967 the International Communications Commission of which Australia was an active member met in Geneva to discuss a co-ordinated scheme for radio communication throughout the world. The historic decision was made that so-called 'Single Side-Band' operation be adopted everywhere, the decision being applicable to almost every country in the world at that time. A compulsory plan was accordingly adopted that the prevailing 'Double Side-Band' operation be phased out by December 1977.

The Flying Doctor Service was faced with a mammoth task. Twelve mother stations had to be completely re-equipped as well as 5000 outback transceivers.

For the first time in Flying Doctor history the radio operators from the 12 base stations were called together by the federal committee to participate in a training conference held in Kilkenny Technical College, Adelaide in May 1972. Don Sandercock of the Broken Hill base later made a recording of this 'thrilling experience'. Never before had it happened in the past 40 years. He made frank reference to the unique place that the radio officer ('the odd men out') really held in keeping the Flying Doctor Service going. To meet Alf Traeger in his 78th year, to share together the whole Australia-wide adventure of introducing the single side-band era, and to keep alive the family spirit of John Flynn the founder – it was an unforgettable happening.

Fred Hull, the senior radio man from Western Australia, spent a whole day with Traeger discussing the inevitable radio events that had overtaken the total service. The Electronic Instrument and Lighting Company (EILCO), allied with the Codan subsidiary company, had since 1961 become a supplier of updated equipment to several Flying Doctor bases and in 1970 had won the contract to modernise all the base installations with updated single side-band equipment. This included transmitters, remote receivers, emergency call systems, radio links and aerials. The tender price of $547,000 was met by the Commonwealth Government. The EILCO company had also undertaken to manufacture 1200 new single side-band outstation sets for sale to network users. Traeger nodded his head as Hull and he 'boiled the billy' together in the Marryatville workshop. They laughed as they recalled events in the adventuring story of the Traeger Transceiver days – the story that they knew was now coming to its final chapter.

However, before his factory closed its doors in 1974 Traeger set out to consummate the dream that had spurred him on from the beginning. He called 'the boys' together at their benches in the old-time honoured workshop. He was determined that Traeger Transceivers Pty Ltd would perform a special final act – and build 20 high-quality single side band transceivers to be offered to needy people in parts of the bush where he had first worked. Thirteen of these expertly constructed sets with the familiar 'Traeger Transceiver' name plate upon them were ordered by Flynn's successor in the Australian Inland Mission. Traeger quietly said: "I want the first one to go to the nursing sisters at Birdsville.' On 23rd September 1973 Sisters Janice Johnson and Sue Rabone, following in the train of Sister Gwen Pearson in 1929, were excitedly working their new single side band radio and calling up the Flying Doctor in Charleville. Traeger was satisfied. His typical smile told its own story.

The Central Section of the Flying Doctor Service helped with the financial management of Traeger's workshop in its final days, but it was inevitable that closing down time was imminent.

In the middle of the next year, 1974, Traeger consulted his doctor. Malignant cancer had invaded his lithe and active body. Just like his old boss John Flynn. With the well-seasoned fountain pen that he had used on the road in 1927 he started to document his personal experiences. He wrote several highly important pages tinged with fun and humour. But the old 'light on the hill' was gradually fading. He gave up his writing. Other more urgent matters were on hand.

CHAPTER SIXTEEN

'Traeger Is Dead'

On Friday 1st August 1980 approximately 6000 Flying Doctor transceivers throughout Australia heard the solemn announcement 'Traeger is dead'.

The 'pedal wireless man', 85 years of age, had died the previous day in his home at Kadonga Avenue, Rosslyn Park, Adelaide.

Alfred Hermann Traeger died as he lived – with quiet dignity and behind the scenes. Joyce, caring and loving wife, had nursed him at home as he faced the losing battle against cancer.

He was a man of quiet Christian faith all his days. At the end there came a great peaceful serenity. Holy Communion on his death bed was a final triumphant act at the hands of his special friend the Luteran pastor. His work was done. He had the exultant feeling that he was travelling again in the old Dodge Buckboard – going home!

This humble and reserved radio 'ham' who shunned praise, who recoiled from shouting crowds, has as many public memorials as the famous Marconi. Two Flying Doctor aircraft carry his name. 'Traeger Park' in Alice Springs is a community facility for hundreds of people. At the Alice Springs Airport overseas travellers stop to be photographed beside the uniquely designed bronze direction-finder that commemorates Traeger's achievements. There is an impressive stone memorial at Glenlee in the Dimboola Shire in Victoria where he was born. Traeger memorabilia are on display at all R.F.D.S. bases. At John Flynn Place in Cloncurry, Traeger is honoured in the imposing 'Traeger Cultural Centre', while within the Flying Doctor Museum there is a professional collection of historic Traeger original pedal wireless sets and equipment.

He made it possible for Flying Doctors to bring security and peace of mind to thousands of people.

Other specially designed memorials are 'Traeger Cottage' in the Old Timers' Homes, Alice Springs, 'Traeger Place' in Cook University Townsville, and the historic stone 'Traeger Cairn' at Port Augusta Flying Doctor Base.

But Traeger's greatest memorial is in the trusted affection which he gathered in the hearts of isolated people in the Australian outback. The young man who looked like a farm hand in work a day trousers and striped braces finally became the 'wireless wizard' who gave a voice to the silent bush, and who made it possible for Flying Doctors to bring medical security and peace of mind to thousands of people.

BIBLIOGRAPHY

Australian National Library. A.I.M. – FRONTIER SERVICES COLLECTION MS5574.

Behr, John. THE RADIO HISTORY OF THE ROYAL FLYING DOCTOR SERVICE.

Electronics Australia. ELECTRONICS AUSTRALIA MAGAZINE (various copies).

Grant, Arch. CAMEL TRAIN AND AEROPLANE.

Idriess, Ion. FLYNN OF THE INLAND.

McPheat, W. Scott. JOHN FLYNN, APOSTLE TO THE INLAND.

Page, Michael. THE FLYING DOCTOR STORY 1928-78.

Proeve, Henry. GOTTLIEB AND HEDWIG SCHULTZ OF WALTON.

Shawsmith, Alan. HALCYON DAYS.

Wilson, George. THE FLYING DOCTOR STORY.

Wireless Institute of Australia. AMATEUR RADIO JOURNAL (various copies).

Woldendorp, Richard. McDonald Roger. AUSTRALIA'S FLYING DOCTORS.

APPENDIX

How the technical story of Traeger's Pedal Wireless unfolded

APPENDIX 1

How Flynn and Traeger brought the first radio equipment to the outback

Flynn's famous Dodge Buckboard played a distinctive role in the adventuring story of Traeger's pedal wireless. In the period 1925-1933 it registered thousands of miles in bush travel in connection with pioneering radio experiments and the installation and servicing of the earliest pedal wireless sets.

A brief description of the Dodge Buckboard (in pre-metric terms) is as follows: Vehicle No. A 221782. Engine No. A 294116. Painted black with movable canvas hood. Tyres 33" x 4.5". Registration SA 43717. Cost Price with pulley on rear wheel £414.

The vehicle was ordered and purchased by Rev. John Flynn from Weymouth Motor Co. Ltd. 42 Weymouth Street, Adelaide on 19th May 1925.

The term 'Buckboard' was the outback name for the so-called country model utility with its loading body constructed of timber in the shape of a well-type tray.

In the text of the Alfred Traeger story the various field adventures of the Dodge Buckboard are part of the rugged romance connected with the creation of Flynn's 'Mantle of Safety'. At the close of its working life with the A.I.M. the vehicle was sold to Mr. Thomas the bookkeeper of Corinda cattle station near Burketown in North Queensland on 1st October 1933. It is understood that its final journey was to some destination 'in the south'. The search for the authentic remains of this historic vehicle has produced considerable archival interest but no practical success in discovering its final location.

Camping gear, food, water, petrol, coir matting to get over sand-hills and the carefully packed experimental radio equipment made up a queer and cumbersome load, with the aerial poles strapped along the passenger side. A 600 volt generator was packed near the tail board. Transmission power for the radio was produced by jacking up the off-side rear wheel on which was a specially constructed pulley for driving the generator.

This was the way John Flynn took the first radio equipment over the notorious Cobbler Track to Innamincka and then through the sandhill country bordering on the Simpson Desert. This was how the whole story of the pedal wireless started.

APPENDIX 2

How Traeger wrote a letter to the A.I.M. Head Office when he was making final preparations to get on the road to Augustus Downs to install Pedal Wireless Set No. 1

AERIAL MEDICAL SERVICE,
FRONTIER NURSING HOMES
AND PATROLS,
BOOKS AND MAGAZINES,
RADIO RELAY LEAGUE.

Presbyterian Church of Australia. Mr. Traeger

A.I.M. Frontier Service Gulf Patrol.

The Gulf Base for the A.I.M. Aerial Medical Service and Radio Relay League is in Cloncurry, N.W. Queensland. A.I.M. Headquarters 926, Pitt Street, Sydney, N.S.W.
Letters for Rev. G. M. Scott may be addressed to either of the following, from which they are forwarded in due course—
Box 103, Cloncurry, N.W. Queensland.
Box 100 C.C. G.P.O., Sydney, N.S.W.

Cloncurry
30 - 5 - 29

Dear Miss Baird

The wireless licences received here, and the reason we wanted them is to check the call signs, and also, as they have to be renewed next month, we can easily attend to this from here, and save the office any inconvenience.

There is an item for expenses which I had almost forgotten, namely rail fares from Duaringa to Longreach.

Please send my next salary payment to Cloncurry.

The wireless work is progressing favourably and everything points to a very satisfactory season.

Yours sincerely

A H Traeger

APPENDIX 3

How Traeger explained the technical details of his original Pedal Wireless

THE RECEIVER consisted of two valves, one detector, one audio, using tetrode tubes type Philips A141. The filament power was supplied by a 1.5-volt large-type dry cell, through a rheostat, the consumption being about .15 amp for both valves.

The plate power was from two 4.5-volt C batteries connected in series, the consumption being about three milliamps.

A regenerative circuit was used, the regeneration being controlled by a .00025 mf condenser.

The tuning and reaction coils were wound on a five-centimetre bakelite tube, the ends of each pair of coils being brought out through the ends of the tube, and connected to valve pins, which fitted an ordinary four-pin valve socket, and so by 'plugging in' opposite ends of the tube, wavelength of 100 to 200 and 200 to 500 could be obtained.

Voltmeters were connected to the valve filaments and across the B battery through press-button switches.

Modifications to the Receiver were carried out nine months after installation by the addition of a second valve.

Interior view of original pedal wireless set.

THE TRANSMITTER was crystal controlled using a Philips Type B 205 receiving valve. Bias for the grid was obtained by a choke and resistance, connected in series across the grid and negative of the filament. The filament was supplied by two 1.5-volt dry cells connected in series through a rheostat, the consumption being about .15 amps.

A voltmeter across the filament, in series with a push-button switch indicated when the batteries required renewal, and the aerial current was indicated by a torch globe connected in series with the aerial. The plate coil together with the aerial coupling coil were wound on a five-centimetre bakelite tube, and the tank circuit was turned on by a small midge condenser. A two mf condenser was connected directly across the generator terminals.

The original transmitting frequency was 88 metres (3.4 MHz).

Technical improvements were effected in 1930 and succeeding years.

APPENDIX 4

How Traeger surprised everybody with his invention of the Pedal Generator

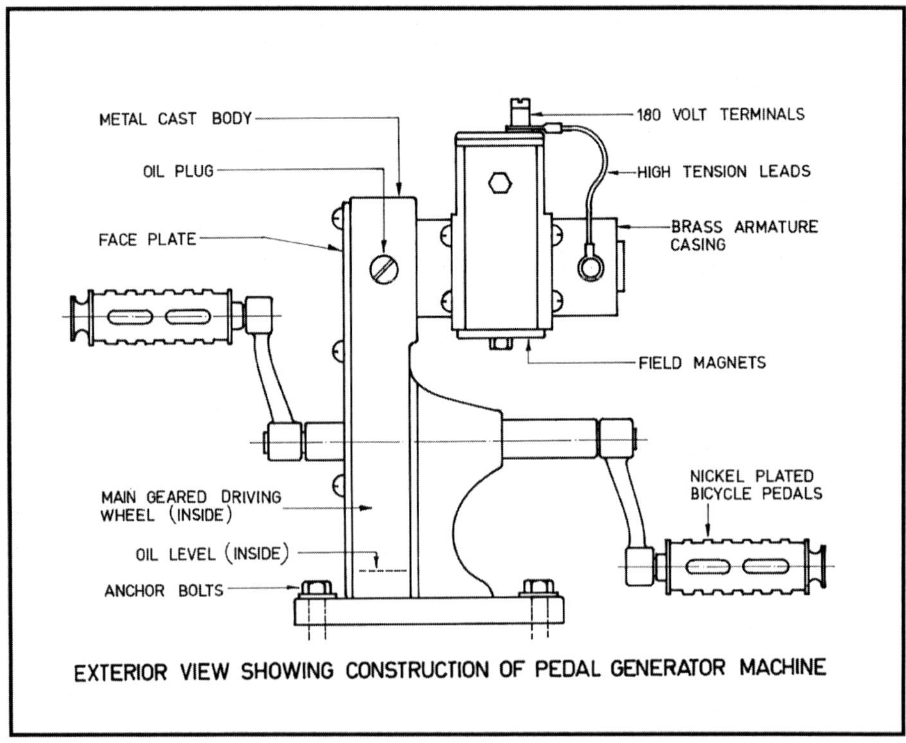

EXTERIOR VIEW SHOWING CONSTRUCTION OF PEDAL GENERATOR MACHINE

The pedal generator was Traeger's miracle device. It meant that electric power became available in outback homes for operating a radio transmitter in a simple, practical way.

The gearing of the machine employed a 192-tooth ring gear 20 centimetres in diameter. It powered a 16-tooth pinion attached to the shaft of the armature at a

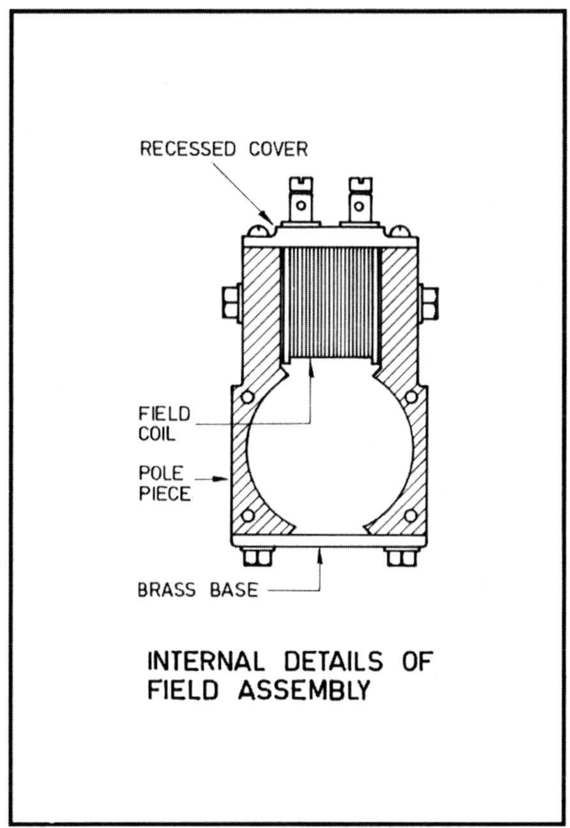

INTERNAL DETAILS OF FIELD ASSEMBLY

drive ratio of 12:1. The gears ran in a bath of SAE 30 lubricating oil. The armature had 13 windings terminating in 26 segments on the commutator end and a caged ball race at the other.

Machine iron castings formed to two pole pieces, which held sufficient residual magnetism to create initial current for the full field. The shunt field coil was a single winding on a three-centimetre-thick iron case with fibre sheets, mounted between the poles. Being in parallel with both source and load, many layers of fine wire were employed to obtain a high impedance of 22K. The field components formed one assembly sitting astride the armature.

Pedalling was carried out at about one revolution per second to spin the armature around 1000 r.p.m. This provided, via the 26-segment commutator, a smooth direct current of 180 volts. There was a slight amount of commutator whine while pedalling.

The original model was painted black. A second slightly improved model was painted battleship grey.

One of the unique relics on display in John Flynn Place, Cloncurry, is No. 1 Pedal Generator used with the original baby set at Augustus Downs in June 1929.

APPENDIX 5

How Traeger took the fears out of Morse code

The Automatic Morse Keyboard

This ingenious machine invented by Alfred Traeger in 1931 resembled a standard four-gang typewriter without the type basket or roller. The case in which it was enclosed was made of metal, strongly braced and securely fastened to a baseboard of Pacific maple wood. The keys were connected to pivoted steel bars with long and short spacings for the necessary 'dots' and 'dashes' of the particular Morse-code letter.

On these arcs there was a bail to activate make-and-break contact points. When a selected key was released the bail was then tripped in synchrony with the appropriate notched spacings. Morse 'dits' and 'dahs' were transmitted with a good ready and smooth flow, with a small, neat, oil-filled drum or dash pot evenly controlling the return of the key.

The keyboard arrangement included all letters of the alphabet, all numerals, and necessary punctuation marks. There were also the radio 'commencement sign' CT, 'pause sign' BT and 'end of message sign' AD.

The keyboard Morse that was transmitted was distinct and uniform.

Traeger records that he built an exact total of 50 of these machines with a slightly improved model in 1933, and they became part of the regular equipment with every baby pedal wireless set in the Cloncurry network until 1935 when telephony units were installed. During that three-year period hundreds of telegrams and medical calls were transmitted on automatic Morse keyboards.

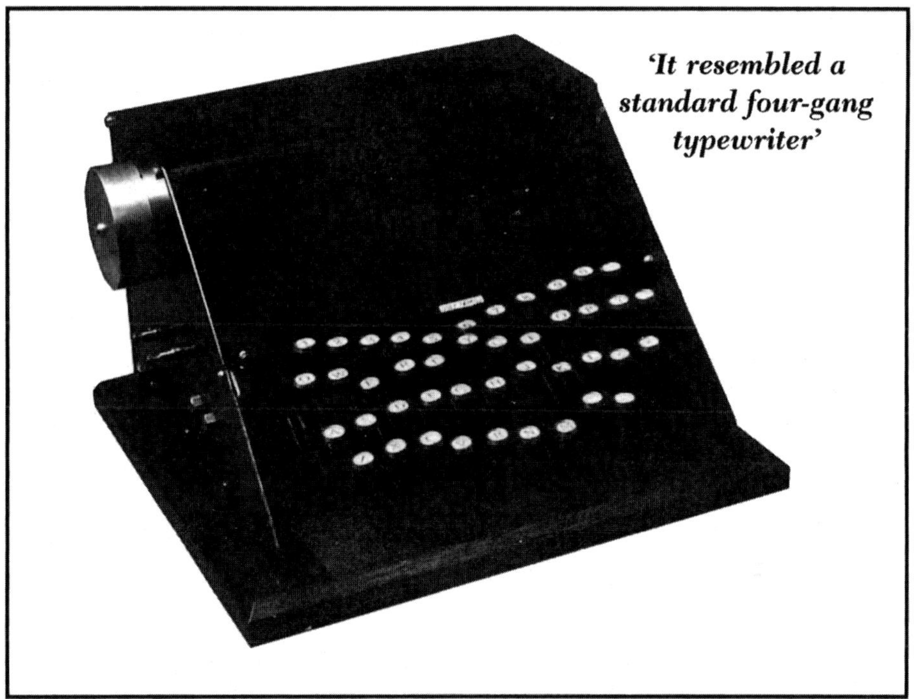

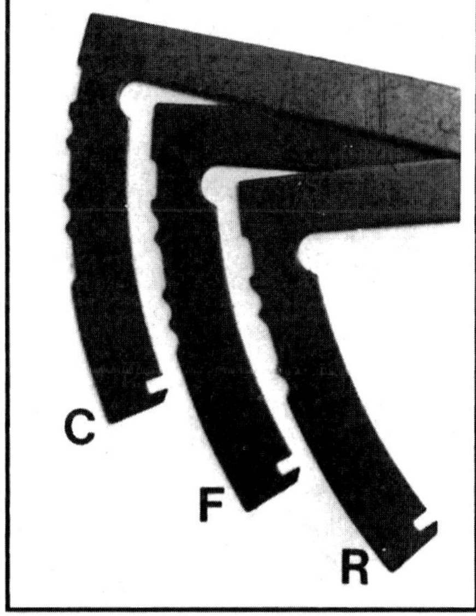

(Above left): Internal view from back of machine illustrating the steel bars with long and short spacings for the particular Morse-code letter and the accompanying oil-filled dash pot to control smooth movement. (Above right): Illustration of the steel arcs with inscribed Morse-code letters. (Photos: Mervyn Eunson)

APPENDIX 6

How Pedal Radio Telegrams tell their own story

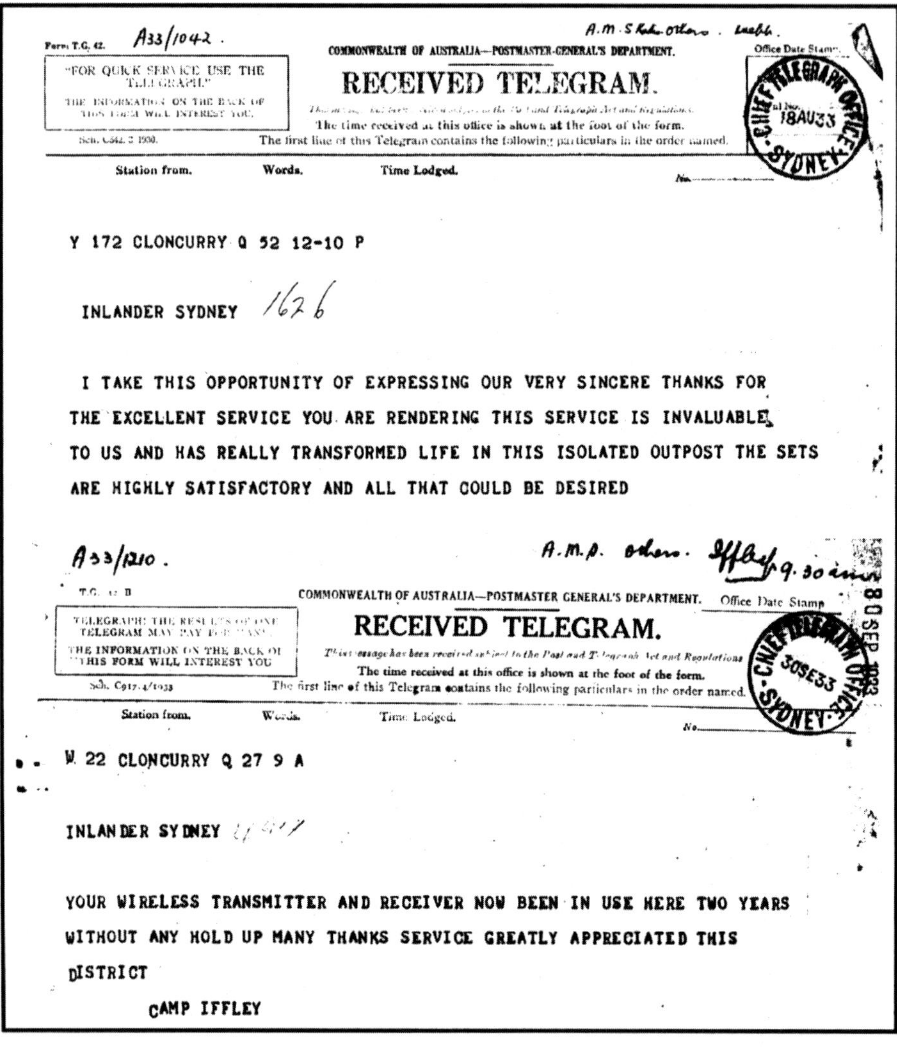

Form T.G. 42. A33/1042. A.M. S... ...

COMMONWEALTH OF AUSTRALIA—POSTMASTER-GENERAL'S DEPARTMENT.

"FOR QUICK SERVICE USE THE TELEGRAPH."
THE INFORMATION ON THE BACK OF THIS FORM WILL INTEREST YOU.

RECEIVED TELEGRAM.

The time received at this office is shown at the foot of the form.
The first line of this Telegram contains the following particulars in the order named.

Office Date Stamp: CHIEF TELEGRAPH OFFICE SYDNEY 18AU33

Station from. Words. Time Lodged. No.

Y 172 CLONCURRY Q 52 12-10 P

INLANDER SYDNEY 1626

I TAKE THIS OPPORTUNITY OF EXPRESSING OUR VERY SINCERE THANKS FOR THE EXCELLENT SERVICE YOU ARE RENDERING THIS SERVICE IS INVALUABLE TO US AND HAS REALLY TRANSFORMED LIFE IN THIS ISOLATED OUTPOST THE SETS ARE HIGHLY SATISFACTORY AND ALL THAT COULD BE DESIRED

A33/1210. A.M.P. ... Iffley 9.30 a.m.

T.G. 12 B

COMMONWEALTH OF AUSTRALIA—POSTMASTER GENERAL'S DEPARTMENT.

TELEGRAPH: THE RESULTS OF ONE TELEGRAM MAY PAY FOR MANY.
THE INFORMATION ON THE BACK OF THIS FORM WILL INTEREST YOU

RECEIVED TELEGRAM.

The time received at this office is shown at the foot of the form.
The first line of this Telegram contains the following particulars in the order named.

Office Date Stamp: CHIEF TELEGRAPH OFFICE SYDNEY 30SE33

Station from. Words. Time Lodged. No.

W 22 CLONCURRY Q 27 9 A

INLANDER SYDNEY

YOUR WIRELESS TRANSMITTER AND RECEIVER NOW BEEN IN USE HERE TWO YEARS WITHOUT ANY HOLD UP MANY THANKS SERVICE GREATLY APPRECIATED THIS DISTRICT

CAMP IFFLEY

FROM THE COLLECTION IN THE NATIONAL LIBRARY CANBERRA WHERE MANY OF THE ORIGINAL TELEGRAMS SENT BY PEDAL RADIO ARE PRESERVED AS HISTORIC ARCHIVAL ITEMS.

APPENDIX 7

How Traeger made specially designed portable pedal radios for travellers on the road

The original portable set was made by Traeger for Kingsley Partridge, the Centralian Patrol Padre, in 1933. A similar set was made for the South Australian patrol.

They were single-valve transmitters and three-valve receivers. Three later improved models were made in 1936-37. These sets were contained in two wooden boxes of identical dimension, the receiver and transmitter in the top one, and the free-running generator and batteries in the lower one.

The following is a description of the 1936 improved model still in working condition and on display in John Flynn Place, Cloncurry.

The receiver has four valves in a regenerative circuit. It is free running and can be tuned down to the broadcast band as well as the higher frequencies of the Cloncurry Flying Doctor Base (34.7 metres, 58.7 metres, 148 metres). Valves used in the receiver are a Radiotron 32-tetrode valve for RF-amplifier, another 32 for the regenerative detector, a 30-triode for audio driver and a transformer coupled 33-tetrode for speaker output.

Power supply for the receiver comes from B battery dry packs, delivering 90 volts to the plates and 22.5 volts to the screens of the RF-amplifier and detector. Negative bias for grid of the 33-audio output valve is derived from a nine-volt C battery. The two-volt filaments of the valves are supplied by two large cylindrical No. 9 dry cells of 1.5 volts connected in series.

The three-valve transmitter uses a Radiotron 49-tetrode as a Pierce oscillator, which is keyed directly for CW signals. Special attention is given to telephone capability by using a 30-triode as microphone pre-amplifier, transformer coupled through a double triode 19-valve to the 49-oscillator/final.

High tension for plate supply of the 49-transmitter valve comes from the 180-volt direct-current pedal generator that is built into the lower box. The transmitter coils are wound on a plug-in former, which also contains the open slab crystal in a plated metal cylinder along with the tuning capacitator and the tuning lamp. Transmitter tuning is achieved by adjusting the tuning capacitator for maximum brightness in a three-volt torch globe in series with the aerial. The set is designed to use a random-length aerial with a close-to-ground counterpoise. Power output of the transmitter is approximately 1.5 watts into the aerial.

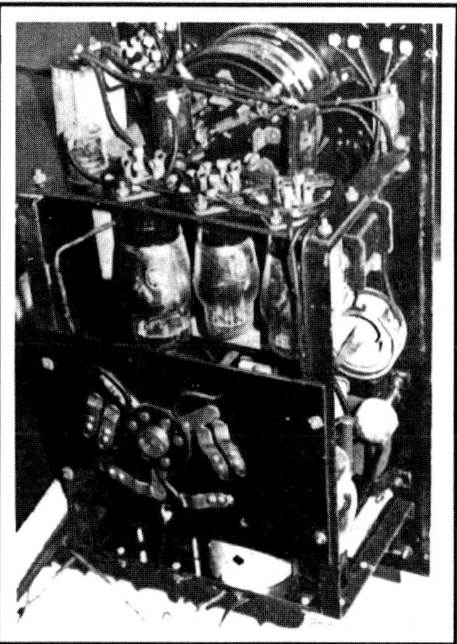

(Above left): Margaret McKay operating portable set on road. (Above right): Interior view of Traeger portable pedal wireless (1936 model).

The 54MC portable pedal set. Even in later years Traeger built a selected number of portable pedal sets for travellers and drovers.

APPENDIX 8

How Traeger made improvements on his Pedal Wireless

Vibrator Power Supplies

Traeger initially invented the pedal generator to produce essential high tension for the bush transmitters because there was no source of electrical power. But when good car batteries came into common use even in remote regions he quickly started to use their new source of power for all the newer sets of transceivers in the field. High tension from vibrator power supplies brought the so-called Traeger vibrator set into production in 1939.

The basic vibrator itself was simply an iron-cored wire coil forming an electromagnet, which acted on a flexible trembler reed fitted with contact points to interrupt the primary supply from the car battery. As the reed vibrated the continuous make and break of the contacts varied the value of applied current through the coil. This pulsating low-voltage current was applied to a step-up transformer to obtain output at a higher voltage. When rectified and filtered the transformer output became high-tension direct current.

In practice, Traeger used a superior type of synchronous vibrator, where two reeds in tandem bore separate sets of contact points. The second set of points, installed in the transformed output circuit, dispensed with the need for rectifier valves.

The vibrator power supply not only furnished high-tension for the transmitter but also for the receiver valves as well, thus eliminating costly dry cell B batteries. Neither were bulky A batteries needed for the heavy drain of valve filaments as the updated sets employed a newer valve type with six-volt filaments that ran directly off the high-capacity car battery.

The Vibrator Set introduced a new era in outback communications with both pedal generators and dry batteries outmoded. In the immediate post-war days all Traeger sets featured vibrator power supplies. From 1959 onwards his later models incorporated solid-state converters, still relying on the vibrator principle but substituting power transistors for the vibrator unit.

One of Traeger's greatest satisfactions was to make School of the Air lessons possible for youngsters in the bush camps. Mr. Tom Cole, a boring contractor, is drilling for artesian water in the Tennant Creek area (Northern Territory). In their bush camp Tom's wife Alia carries on with the 'housework' while Barry has his regular School of the Air lessons on a Traeger vibrator wireless set. (Photo: News and Information Bureau)

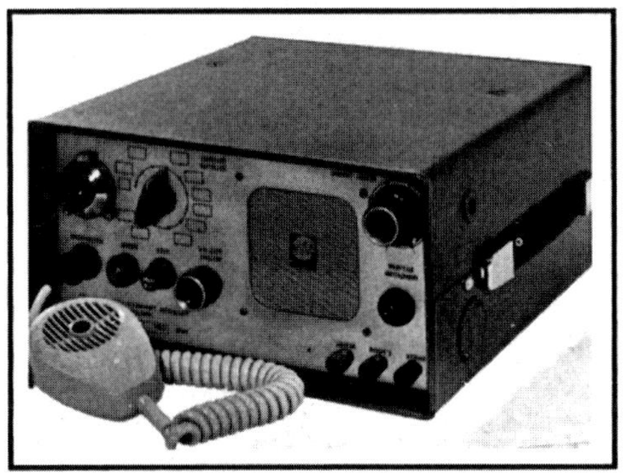

The popular vibrator model (CM7) of the 1960s. Traeger still using the vibrator principle but now incorporating solid-state converters and power transistors.

APPENDIX 9

How Traeger made it possible for the Flying Doctor to hold medical consultations while in flight

Model of the original de Havilland 50A Aircraft now housed as a unique archival exhibit in John Flynn Place, Cloncurry. In this historic ambulance aeroplane Alfred Traeger, with the assistance of Maurie Anderson, radio operator, built and installed the miracle wireless equipment that enabled Flying Doctor Jock Rossell in 1934, for the first time in medical history, to carry out air-to-ground consultations. In the background is a modern Flying Doctor aircraft, a Super King Air 200, with world-scale radio equipment that has evolved from the pioneering work of Traeger.

APPENDIX 10

How the 'Single Side Band' revolution happened

The International Communications Commission affecting most countries in the world including Australia issued a mandatory order that all communication agencies change to single side-band operation by certain dates.

The single side-band system is complex technically but the following is a general description of how SSB evolved.

In the beginning of radio science the emission was a damped waveform generated by an induction spark coil. There was only one mode of operation. The full power of the carrier emission was simply keyed to form Morse telegraphy messages.

Thermionic valves later gave a better means of generating the carrier. Unlike spark sets, the waveform of the valve emission was a continuous wave. So radio-telegraphy using valves was termed CW mode.

The technology of valves also allowed a form of voice radio telephony by superimposing the low audio frequencies of speech on the high-frequency radio carrier wave. As the carrier was modified or modulated by the amplitude of speech frequencies, this radio telephony was termed amplitude modulation or AM mode.

But in practice AM technology proved manifestly deficient and ineffective compared with CW. It also involved greater complexity and expense. For reliable long-distance communication the efficient Morse transmissions of CW remained the favoured mode.

The deficiency of AM arises in that about two-thirds of transmitted power is contained in the carrier, which in AM serves only as a vehicle for the speech frequency sidebands. The AM mode is otherwise wasteful in occupying excessive

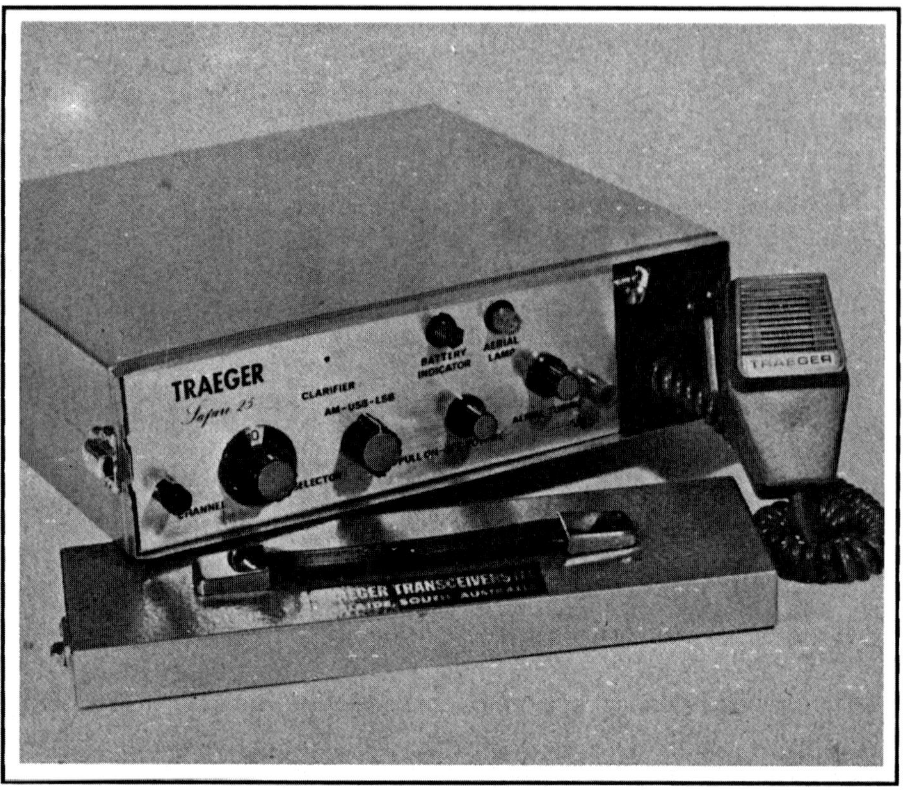

Traeger's workshop turned out a series of single side-band sets in the early 1970s such as The Safari 25. When the contract was impending for the Australia-wide installation of single side-band in the 12 R.F.D.S. bases it was beyond the capacity of the Traeger team to match this total task. Eilco won the contract.

band width to accommodate the full range of speech frequencies. Both defects are overcome by modifying the transmission.

Such modified form of AM produce the so-called side-band modes. Firstly, by eliminating the carrier the full transmitted power contains only the two speech side-bands to form double side-band or DSB mode. The efficiency of the transmitter was therefore greatly increased.

As each speech side-band is a mirror image of the other, either side-band can be suppressed to form a single side-band SSB mode. This again raised transmitter efficiency and also halves the band width for greater use of available band space. The benefit of narrow band width is further enhanced by severely restricting the range of voice frequencies transmitted.

Adoption of single side-band voice transmissions to relieve band congestion became compulsory for all R.F.D.S. radio bases and outpost sets by December 1977. Updated solid-state technology was introduced at the same time leading to extremely efficient modern miniaturised equipment.

In 1972 Traeger offered to build SSB sets for all the field staff of the Australian Inland Mission. Reviving old-time memories he arranged for the despatch of the first one to the nursing sisters at Birdsville. Sisters Janice Johnson (standing) and Sue Roberts (Birdsville Frontier Services Hospital) call up the Charleville Flying Doctor on their No. 1 Traeger single side-band radio. A totally new era in outback communication had begun. Forty-five years earlier the old historic pedal wireless had set the course.

APPENDIX 11

How the legacy of Alfred Traeger lives on

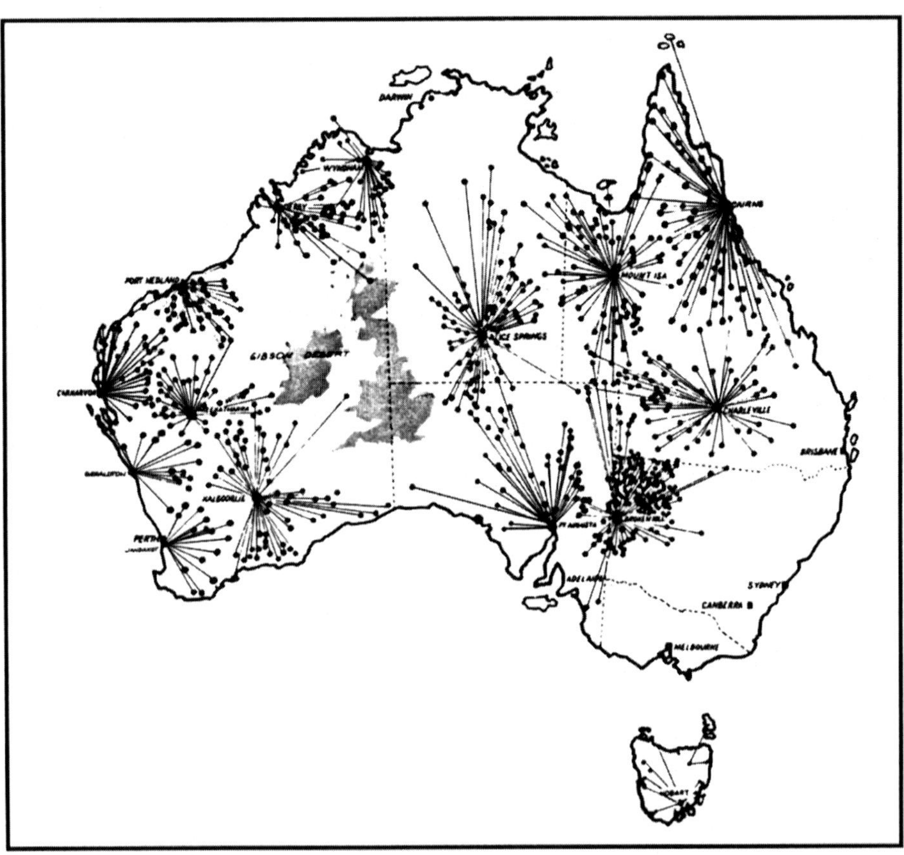

The 'Mantle of Safety' of the modern Royal Flying Doctor Service of Australia is a bonded network of life-saving communication because a man called Alfred Traeger first of all invented a pedal wireless.